HOW TO PUBLISH
YOUR OWN BOOK

HOW TO PUBLISH YOUR OWN BOOK

A GUIDE FOR AUTHORS
WHO PLAN TO PUBLISH
A BOOK AT THEIR OWN EXPENSE

BY L.W. MUELLER

HARLO PRESS
DETROIT, MICHIGAN

HARLO PRESS

16721 Hamilton Avenue   Detroit, Michigan 48203

To my wife, Marion,
and
to the many authors and poets
for whom Harlo Press
has produced books
during the past thirty years
and to those persons
for whom we hope
to produce books in the future.

CONTENTS

1 INTRODUCTION

This book will provide many helpful hints to the aspiring author who is sincerely interested in getting his book, or series of books, into print.

Among other things, it offers advice about manuscript preparation, selecting a book printer, determining the number of books to print, choosing the kind of paper and binding, and techniques for selling books.

It also discusses such things as "vanity" publishers, copyright law, Library of Congress Catalog Book Numbers, and International Standard Book Numbers.

We are all aware that a writer writes books and that some printers print books, but to many persons book *publishing* is somewhat mysterious.

Briefly, the publisher is the person who makes the capital investment. This holds just as true if you, as an individual, take this risk on your own book, as it does with a large trade publisher.

The publisher, thus, takes the gamble, has the book prepared, and then offers it for sale or distribution.

But how?

Very few books have been written on the *entire* subject, although the bibliography lists a number of excellent books that offer help in various areas and cover certain aspects in considerably more depth.

I spend part of nearly every day answering questions about book printing and publishing. Thus it seemed logical to me to digest the pertinent written matter and add information I've learned from practical experience.

You may have noticed that I've switched to the first person. This will happen throughout the book, because much of what is discussed is not drawn from books. And, as I've been associated with Harlo Printing Company for thirty years, I may tend to relate my experiences with those of the company.

So, as you read this book, treat it as though we were having a chat. I'll try to anticipate your questions and answer them as factually and personally as possible.

My introduction to printing took place in 1937, when I studied printing in high school, while also working part-time at two job printing plants. Incidentally, I received the grand sum of eighteen cents per hour at one shop, and twenty-two cents at the other.

After high school, allowing time out for serving as a pilot in the Navy during World War II, I received a Bachelor of Arts Degree in Industrial Education, with a major in printing.

Then came a period of teaching printing in a high school, doing graduate work, and also teaching night school journalism classes in college.

During my teaching days, Harlo Printing Company was born. I shouldn't really say "born." "Hatched" would be a better word, because a former partner and I started with a total investment of $600 (of which I had to borrow my half), in the back end of a barber shop.

This was in 1946. Our total overhead, which included rent, heat, electricity, and the services of the barber, who answered the telephone while we were not there, was $20 per month.

Naturally, Harlo Printing Company has grown considerably during the intervening years. We have moved to larger quarters several times and continually add modern equipment. But, although we are now an extremely efficient shop, and do quality work, we are still small enough so that either by correspondence or personally, we get to know the persons we deal with, and hear the results they obtain from their books.

Because I intend to hit only the high spots, I've included names and addresses (and sometime current prices) of places where additional information is available.

Everything has been thoroughly checked and, so far as I know, is currently correct. But companies come and go; names, addresses, and prices change. So not everything may be up-to-date by the time you read this book. Check if you are in doubt; if you find anything incorrect, let me know. We'll include it in the revised edition.

It is my aim, particularly, to help the relatively inexperienced person, first of all to publish an attractive book; then, if this is his wish, to give him aids that will help him sell more books than he would have been able to sell without help.

—*L. W. Mueller*

2 WHY SHOULD YOU PUBLISH YOUR OWN BOOK?

I don't know how the feeling grew, although no doubt the "vanity" presses (which I'll discuss later) helped the cause along, that publishing one's own book in some way signifies that it is inferior to a book published by a large, commercial "trade" house like Doubleday, Putnam or Random House.

This certainly need not be the case. History has proven otherwise.

I'm not saying that all persons who self-published books were rewarded with fame or made large sums of money, but many are remembered.

Read the biographies or autobiographies of some of the following people; you will find them fascinating:

Nathaniel Hawthorne, John Bartlett, William Blake, Robert Burns, Edgar Rice Burroughs, Lord Byron, Stephen Crane, George Bernard Shaw, Mary Baker Eddy, Thomas Gray, Zane Grey, Elbert Hubbard, Washington Irving,

James Joyce, D. H. Lawrence, Emily Bronte, Charlotte Bronte, Thomas Paine, Edgar Allen Poe, Alfred Lord Tennyson, Ezra Pound, Rudyard Kipling, Henry M. Robert, Henry David Thoreau, Carl Sandburg, Thomas Hardy, Percy Bysshe Shelley, Upton Sinclair, Mark Twain, Horace Walpole, Theodore Dreiser, and Walt Whitman.

The foregoing are only a few of the persons who self-published part or all their work.

The same thing is happening today.

I know that 100 years from now, some of the books produced by Harlo and similar companies will be referred to, and that their authors will still "live," because, like any time in history, these last few decades have produced a unique type of writer.

But, back to you.

You would not have written your manuscript unless you thought it had merit. Because of your convictions, you also feel that other people share your view. This is natural.

Unless you wrote your book for purely personal reasons, realizing that it would have a very limited sales appeal; or, on the other hand, the sales potential is exceptional, chances are that you have tried to have your book published by several of the large commercial houses. I encourage this. But, chances are also good that they have all rejected your manuscript.

Assuming that your manuscript has merit, and is well written, rejection does not mean your manuscript is bad. It may be exceptionally good.

Commercial publishers must sell from 7,000 to 10,000 copies of a book in order to break even. They cannot afford to gamble on an unknown author, or on a manuscript that has a limited sales appeal, no matter how high the quality, or how polished the writing.

This is often the case with poetry. I'll stress again: Quality is not necessarily the determining factor; sales potential is. Although Harlo has printed over 100,000 copies of one poet's works, for a small publisher, this is an exception, not the rule.

Local and regional histories and autobiographies, which I feel are facets of publishing, that for the sake of our heritage, *must* be preserved, are also most often rejected. Yet, in a modest way, if properly promoted, they sell quite well.

Back to the large commercial houses.

After receiving several rejection slips and consuming considerable time—because the large houses have an extremely large backlog of unsolicited material—some authors just give up. But most do not.

They want to see their book in print for a number of reasons. The making of money is often not the sole factor. Prestige in a profession, fame in the local community, the need to pass on to posterity their thoughts or the results of their research, are strong, motivating forces.

The fact that a large commercial house doesn't, won't, or can't afford to publish your manuscript, does not mean *you* can not. Publishing is different from many businesses. The fact that a publisher is *large* does not make him your competitor.

At this stage, some people turn to the "subsidy" or "vanity" press. But, before you go this route, read Chapter 21 thoroughly. Some people, no doubt, have been successful using their services, but many have met with bitter disappointment—often at great financial expense.

I would definitely recommend self-publication at this point. Pick an honest, experienced book printer (Harlo Printing Company is one—there are, of course, others) who is familiar with ways to help the individual who is often publishing his first book.

Remember, most authors have a number of "built-in" sales. They have friends and business associates; they may teach, lecture, or put on demonstrations. They may own a building or historic site that is visited by hundreds of people—all potential customers; or they may decide to put on a vigorous sales campaign of their own, feeling that they will make more money than if they had a commercial house publish their work.

If you only want a limited number of copies produced (I usually recommend 500 or 1000 copies as a sufficient number to test a book), it may be unwise to choose a book printer who specializes in long run printing. He cannot afford to produce limited editions.

On the other hand, you should not choose a printer merely because he is close to you, geographically. Shipping is a minor part of the overall cost.

In many cases you will need help. The book printer you deal with should be able to give you honest, knowledgeable advice about your copyright and Library of Congress Catalog Card Number; help you style your manuscript; be able to "touch up" your grammar, spelling, punctuation and sentence structure, if needed; suggest proper type styles; be able to supply artwork if necessary; recommend suitable paper; explain different kinds of binding; and give you the benefit of his experience when you ask questions or seek advice.

He should also be able to design and produce attractive book covers and dust jackets.

The honest book printer, although sensitive about your undertaking, will not, nor should he, be in a position to evaluate your material as to sales potential. He will do an expert job of printing and binding, in the minimum amount of time necessary to produce an attractive book, and ship the books to you, properly boxed, so they arrive in good condition.

The selling is up to you. You are, in effect, *your own publisher.*

3 HOW TO PREPARE AND MAIL YOUR MANUSCRIPT

The careful physical preparation of your manuscript can save you money. All copy should be typed. It is extremely difficult and costly for a printer to work from handwritten copy. Many people specialize in typing manuscripts. If you cannot locate someone in your community, check the *Writer's Digest* or *The Writer*. These publications regularly print names of people who do this work, together with their rates which, incidentally, are very moderate.

I will emphasize, however, that just because a manuscript *looks* professional, does not mean it is accurate. Although most typists will correct obvious errors in spelling and punctuation, by all means check the typed manuscript several times before submitting it for printing.

You are the author; you know the facts; you should have the manuscript as near perfect as possible before submission.

I would recommend that you use the carbon copy for checking purposes. After you are satisfied that everything is in order, transcribe your revisions to the original copy. Neat, hand-written changes will not hamper the printer too much.

Remember, that once the type is set, your printer will charge for any alterations he has to make.

Introductory Material

A well planned, well printed book will pretty much follow a standard format: there will be preliminary pages, the text, and the end pages.

I'd recommend that you type your name, or pseudonym, and complete *current* address at the top left of the title page. A telephone number, if you don't mind being called (together with the best time to reach you) is also helpful in case the printer has questions.

Following your title page, place all pertinent pages which appear before the actual text of the book. (See Chapter 19, which discusses the parts of your book and the proper order in which to place preliminary, text and end pages.)

Text of the Book

Start the first chapter, and subsequent chapters, about one-third of the way down from the top of the page. *Be sure to indicate chapter number and complete chapter title.*

Although single spacing is acceptable for poetry, the complete text of your book should be *double-spaced* on one side of a white, 8½-by-11-inch sheet, using a black ribbon. The typing should be neat, with a minimum number of corrections or changes. Check dates, names, statements of fact, spelling, punctuation and grammar very carefully. Be sure you have secured written permission, from the owner, if you use copyrighted material.

I am not saying that a printer *will not*, nor *cannot*, work with a manuscript that does not adhere to the preceding suggestions or those which follow, but the work will take him longer and consequently cost you more.

There should be about a one-inch margin all around

the typed page. This will leave space if the printer needs to write instructions. The margins will also allow room for minor changes which result from copyreading and styling.

Keep the line length, number of lines per page, and type size, consistent throughout the manuscript. It is virtually impossible for a printer to estimate the number of pages there will be in the printed book, and the ultimate price, when line lengths, number of lines per page, and type sizes vary.

Use *double,* not triple, spacing between paragraphs. The printer doesn't double-space. Be sure, however, to indent paragraphs about five spaces. Allow extra space (to denote changes of thought, or the like) only if you want it.

If material is to carry an extra indention when printed (quotes, reprints from newspapers, letters), also indent this five spaces, *but double-space it.*

Each page number should be consecutively numbered from front to back—not by chapter—and should carry your last name at the top of each page. Picture what could happen if one of your pages was inadvertently misplaced in a print shop where the printer may be working on dozens of manuscripts at one time.

MAILING YOUR MANUSCRIPT

If the manuscript is short, it can be mailed in a sturdy 9-by-12-inch clasp envelope. For longer manuscripts, the boxes in which typing paper comes, make handy mailing cartons.

Do not staple pages together or put them in a binder. The printer must take them apart anyway.

Book manuscripts can be mailed at a special rate of 21 cents for the first pound and 9 cents for each additional pound, providing the statement "Special Fourth Class Rate —Books," is added to the outside of the parcel. If you wish to include a letter, add "First Class Letter Enclosed" on the front and an additional 13 cents postage. (Remember, postage rates change; these are current.)

Be sure to attach your complete return address. The

Post Office will not return mail to you unless the statement "Return Postage Guaranteed" is affixed, and you pay the return cost upon receipt.

The special book rate, even with a First Class letter enclosed, takes considerably longer to arrive, than First Class or Air Mail.

It may pay you to send at the latter rates, even though the cost is greater. It is also a practical idea to insure your parcel and send it by Registered Mail.

Always Keep a Copy

There is always the possibility that a manuscript might get lost, so it is a good idea to keep a carbon copy or have a copy made on a copying machine. It is wise, however, to send the printer the original. Some copies are poor, and if the printer has to spend time interpreting whether an "o" is really an "e," he wastes time, and is more likely to make errors.

Artwork, Photographs and Captions

Never paste artwork or photographs to your manuscript pages. Keep them separate. When mailing artwork or photographs wrap the package securely to make sure it doesn't bend and damage, particularly, the edges of the contents.

Captions should be typed on a separate sheet of paper and should *not* be affixed to artwork or photographs. Number your captions (Example: Illustration 1, page 28 of manuscript), and put a corresponding number on the back of the artwork or photograph, together with your name. This same number can be inserted in the margin of the manuscript at the exact or approximate position you want the illustration to appear. And, don't press too hard on the back of photographs or artwork. The impression can show through on the front. Never cut down photographs, even though only a portion of the area is to be used; rather, write instructions on the back of the photograph or indicate the area to be used by employing crop marks.

A printer can't work miracles. Although other finishes

will be accepted, a glossy photograph, with a lot of contrast (white whites, and black blacks), makes the best reproduction.

Colored photographs can be reproduced in black and white with fair success, but special, more costly, camera techniques must be employed, and the results are more unpredictable.

The age of a photograph is not necessarily a determining factor. Photos from family albums, even when old, that are sharp and clear, reproduce well if they do not have to be enlarged too much.

Most modern printers also use techniques that will reproduce photographs that have already been printed, with a fair degree of success.

Line work (material which has no tones) reproduces excellently, and if furnished to the exact size it is to appear when printed, adds little to the cost if the book is printed by offset.

If you have a choice, furnish photographs and line work oversize rather than undersize. Reducing will sharpen detail; enlargement will magnify defects.

It is wise to ask the printer's opinion if you have any doubt whether a particular photograph or piece of art will reproduce well. If it is questionable, he can "shoot" the artwork and supply you with a silverprint which will give you a pretty good idea of how it will look when printed. The cost for this is moderate.

A SIMPLE METHOD OF ESTIMATING THE NUMBER OF PAGES

4

The body type for this book is set in 11 point (pt.) Times Roman, 1 point (pt.) leaded.

For comparison, the paragraphs describing how to estimate the number of pages if your manuscript is poetry, are set in 12 point (pt.) Garamond, 2 points (pts.) leaded. Both are set 23 picas wide; 40 picas deep.

I'll confine the explanation to these two type faces. Using the formula that follows, your printer should be able to give you the approximate number of words per page for any given type style and line length.

Estimating Number of Pages
if Your Manuscript Is Prose

In order to estimate the number of pages your manuscript will make when printed, you must first determine the number of words in your text.

1. Count the number of words in 10 typical *full* lines

on a number of typical pages, and divide by 10. *This will give you the average number of words per line.*

2. Determine the number of *lines* on a *typical* full page. Count *all* lines, whether there is one word on the line or whether the line is full.

3. Count the number of pages in the entire text.

4. Multiply the number of words per line, times the number of lines per page, times the number of pages. For the purpose of the formula which follows, this will give you the number of words in the text of your manuscript.

5. *For 11 pt. type, 1 pt. leaded,* set the width and depth of this page, divide your total number of words by 375. *For 12 pt. type, 2 pts. leaded,* set the width and depth of this page, divide your total number of words by 325. This will give you the number of printed pages in the text.

6. As not all chapter endings come out as full pages, and the beginnings of chapters normally start down from the top, add ½ page for each chapter.

7. If additional pages appear after the text, allow for these pages.

8. Add for the half title, the title page, copyright page, acknowledgments, contents and other preliminary pages. Remember that most preliminary pages usually begin as right-hand pages, so allow the necessary blank pages. Preliminary and back pages are discussed in Chapter 19.

9. Most printers print in multiples of 16 pages (64, 80, 96, 112, etc.), so for purposes of estimating it is wise to assume that your book will print out to the next higher number of pages divisible by 16. (Example: If you come out to 90 pages, use 96 pages for estimating purposes.)

Your printer will scale your manuscript as accurately as possible before quoting prices.

Estimating Number of Pages
if Your Manuscript Is Poetry

Allow a maximum of 37 lines per page. Don't forget that spaces between stanzas count as one line, the title counts as one line, and the space below the title counts as one line. Also, don't forget to allow for especially long lines that will have to be printed as two lines by the printer.

I do not recommend cramming your poetry into a book. Poems, unless very short, look better if each begins on a new page.

To the total number of pages of poetry add for the preliminary and back pages, as discussed previously in Point 8.

5 SETTING PRINT QUANTITY, SIZE, AND PRICE OF YOUR BOOK

You should give careful consideration to the number of copies you decide to print, the size of your finished book, and the price.

HOW MANY BOOKS SHOULD I HAVE PRINTED?

The *per book* cost drops in relation to the number of copies printed; the more copies printed at one time, the less cost per copy.

Let's take a general case, using hypothetical prices to illustrate the point. *Relative* prices for a hardbound book could be about as follows: 250 copies—$1105 ($4.42 per book); 500 copies—$1245 ($2.49 per book); 1000 copies—$1585 ($1.58 per book); 5000 copies—$4150 (83¢ per book).

You can readily see the relationship.

Be Conservative

Cost per copy, however, is not the sole determining factor. Books are much harder to sell than the relatively inexperienced person realizes.

Never order more books than you realistically think you can sell.

Unless you pretty well *know* the potential sales before the books are printed, be conservative. Not all books, even those published by the large firms, succeed.

Treat your original printing as a test. A rerun at a later date will cost considerably less than the first printing.

From my experience, I would say that an initial printing of 1000 copies is normally enough to test the market. Even 1000 copies may be too many for some books.

Keep an Eye on Results
of Prepublication Advertising

Read very carefully Chapters 10 and 11, that discuss promotion.

While your book is being typeset, you should be actively engaged in your sales campaign. If prospects look good, you can always increase the quantity any time prior to the beginning of actual printing. If you decide that it would be better to reduce the initial order, you should have no trouble doing so, providing the printer has not had to order special body or cover paper or special cover cloth. Be frank with him; the honest printer will cooperate with you.

WHAT SIZE BOOK
SHOULD I ORDER?

For most conventional books, I would recommend a 5½" x 8½" size for hardbound and saddle stitched books and a 5⅜" x 8½" size for perfect-bound books. (Perfect binding requires that ⅛" be trimmed off the gutter edge of the paper.)

These sizes have eye-appeal and fit most book and library shelves. They are also practical when it comes to printing and binding costs.

Books are normally printed on large sheets containing 16 or 32 pages, which are then folded down to size prior to binding.

The 5½" x 8½" size book fits standard-size paper and press sizes, and can be conveniently, economically, and attractively bound.

If your manuscript demands large-size maps, diagrams, or illustrations, I'd recommend, although a bit cumbersome in many cases, an 8½" x 11" book.

Alternate sizes to the 5½" x 8½" and 8½" x 11" book are the 6" x 9" and 9" x 12" book. More and more American presses, however, are manufactured which suit 5½" x 8½" or multiples thereof.

Remember, if the printer you choose has equipment that efficiently prints 5½" x 8½" or 8½" x 11" books, demanding a 6" x 9" or 9" x 12" book, may cut his press productivity by as much as 50%.

Many authors request prices for 4¼" x 7" books. This is the approximate size for paperbacks which are sold by the millions in drugstores and newsstands.

This sounds, and may be practical, from a distribution standpoint—if you can get a company to distribute your book over a large enough area. But, from a price and profit standpoint, it may be impractical.

The standard, mass-*distributed* paperback is also mass-*produced,* and thus the unit cost per book is extremely low. This is why, even with the hundreds of thousands of books that are never sold, the publisher of mass-produced paperbacks can survive. Remember, also, that in most cases, it has been the hardbound book that was advertised, received the rave reviews, and created the demand for the paperback.

Much of the cost for producing comparatively short run books is involved with typesetting and otherwise getting the book ready to print, so you can never effectively compete, so far as price goes, with a mass-produced book.

This is why there are two general classifications of softbound books: the higher priced, 5½" x 8½" or thereabout, non-newsstand-size book which people are accustomed to paying higher prices for, and the mass-produced, approximately 4¼ " x 7" book.

But, if you want to gamble on later mass sales, you might try the following approach.

First, contact a distributor in your area, telling him of your plans to publish a newsstand-size paperback and get his guarantee that he will distribute it. Chances are that he will want a 50% discount.

Then put out an attractive book with sales appeal. Most paperbacks are sold by the cover. Your book, no doubt, will be superior so far as inside paper, readability and typesetting are concerned (most mass-produced paperback books lack attractive design), so this is a plus.

Price it competitively. Remember this is a test to see whether the book will sell.

If you have a good response, you are in business.

Be sure that your printer guarantees that all negatives or reproduction proofs are *your* property.

If your book is successful, even in a limited test area, contact another distributor: Tell him what happened in the first area. After all, he is interested in making money.

If you receive successful results in several areas, contact one of the large paperback publishers. Give him the *exact* facts: Such and such company in such and such city did a test on my book and sold so many percent in so many months. Tell him that the book is already typeset and that you own all rights, and can furnish negatives or reproduction proofs.

Chances are good that you will lose money on the original printing, but it *might* be worth a gamble.

WHAT SHOULD I CHARGE
FOR MY BOOK?

Every book is unique. There is nothing else like it on the market. Thus, in theory, if you present a book to a prospective purchaser which he cannot buy anywhere else, he will pay any amount in order to obtain it, providing the subject is of interest to him.

On the other hand, you must be aware of competition. Most people will only pay what they consider a fair price. But, let me stress that a dollar or two difference will not affect sales to a great extent. *Do not underprice your book* in the hope of increasing sales.

Large publishers charge anywhere from four to eight times the actual cost of producing a book. But their printings are large. They *have* to be large. They will not publish a manuscript that does not warrant a large printing.

So, be realistic. I'd recommend browsing in a bookstore, if you haven't done so recently. The price of books has jumped considerably. Paper prices have doubled in the past few years, and other production costs have gone up in proportion.

Also, remember that the price printed on your book is not necessarily what you are going to receive for it.

If you are planning to sell through bookstores, or through a wholesaler, you must allow for their discount. Because they work on a percentage of the retail price, they are more likely to push a higher priced book. These discounts are discussed elsewhere.

Also, if it is your intention to sell your book, and make a profit, you must allow for adequate promotion, the cost of review copies, spoilage, and in some cases, storage.

Remember, Your Book Is Unique!

You know your book is unique. Why not make it even more so? I don't know if the same thing happens to you, but I get a thrill when I see a book that contains a statement somewhat like the following:

> This, the first edition
> of this book, has been
> limited to five hundred copies.
> This is book No. _____

And, I'm more likely to purchase it!

What is wrong with mentioning this in your prepublication offer? Or, why not guarantee that all orders received will be autographed by the author?

What will Number 98 of an autographed, limited edition copy of your book be worth in a few years? I'm not necessarily speaking of money. What pride will your friends, children or grandchildren feel?

6 HOW TO PREPARE THE COVER OR JACKET OF YOUR BOOK

The primary reasons for putting a cover on your book (if your book is softbound) or using a jacket (if your book is hardbound) are two-fold:

1. To aid you in selling your book.
2. To protect your book.

Although covers and dust jackets are physically different, they have many things in common. The trite saying, "You can't judge a book by its cover," may be true, but the fact remains that when a person is browsing in a bookstore, a colorful, attractive, quick-attention-getting, dramatic cover, is bound to attract his eye faster than a drab one.

Picture your book jacket or cover as a poster which advertises your book. Convince the prospective purchaser that there is no substitute for your book.

Remember, you have only a split-second to sell the customer; therefore, the first thing to bear in mind is to design the cover (or jacket) so you will get the potential

purchaser's *immediate* attention. This means the *back* cover
as well as the front and spine. You never know how a book
will be displayed.

An attractive cover does not necessarily add to the expense. With the introduction of new photographic typesetting equipment employed by modern printers, type styles
and sizes are virtually unlimited. Often, dramatic results
can be obtained, merely by using unusual type faces, bright
colors, tints or reverses.

Remember that the top and bottom edges of the cover
of a hardbound book will show even if the jacket is on, so
use colors which, even though different, are compatible.

Front Cover and Spine

Naturally, the title, which should be intriguing, and the
name of the author, should be prominently displayed on the
cover and spine in a clear, readable manner.

I heard one publisher state, and I think wisely, that the
lettering on the spine should be large enough so that it can
be easily read whether the book is displayed on the top
or bottom shelf of a book store.

Often a sub-heading, or cover blurb, will help sell a
book. This is applicable even if the title is self-explanatory.

Suppose your title is *Bargain Vacation Spots in Ameri-
ca*. Embellishing the title with a statement like: "100 Spots
Where You Can Spend the Night for Under $8," "Get More
Than Twice for Your Money," or "An Island Where You
Can Live for $30 a Week," will help sell the book.

If the title is not self-explanatory, for instance, *Dramatic Encounter,* add an explanation such as, "A Sailor's
Odyssey," "The True Facts Concerning Howard Jones,"
or "The Biography of an Ex-Slave."

Stress the fact that the buyer is getting his money's
worth. Study the current "best sellers." You will find that
they invariably follow these guide lines.

The cover should also list the selling price in a con-
spicuous place. The best location for the price of a softbound book is on the front cover. If a jacket is used, the
price should appear at the top of the inside front flap. If you

anticipate price changes, the price can be left off when printing, and you can add a small label indicating price.

Back Cover

Don't forget that the back cover is also important. Again, the aim is to attract attention.

A photograph of the author, along with biographical material, is one proper approach. But don't let vanity alone dictate this decision. Perhaps statements about the book from authorities will do a better selling job. If you don't have quotes for your current book, you may have quotes from previously published books. Or, for a bit of shock, the front cover can be reproduced in its entirety on the back, or the front cover can continue on the back. Remember, you don't know how the book will be displayed.

You can also use the back cover, or inside back cover, to list other books you have written, or titles projected for the future. This is a good way to get additional orders.

The Library of Congress Catalog Card Number and International Standard Book Number, if you have one, may also be placed on the back cover. The name and address of where books may be ordered should *definitely* be included, either on the back or one of the inside flaps.*

Flaps of Dust Jackets
and Inside Covers of Softbound Books

Here is another chance for selling. Most often flaps of jackets contain copy, but often people tend to overlook the selling potential of the inside covers of softbound books. The same things apply.

Naturally, what you put on the inside is somewhat dependent on what you have on the back. But, very commonly, a short, no-nonsense, synopsis of the book is in-

---

*In the case of Harlo Press, if we produce a book under our imprint, we automatically forward any orders sent to us, to the author for filling. We request that the author furnish us with self-addressed, stamped envelopes.

cluded on the inside front flap of a jacket. The copy should be concise, and should attract attention. It may be continued on the inside back flap.

This synopsis need not be in paragraph form. It may, for instance, list the most unique things about the book, the contents, or the like.

If not used on the back, facts about the author, with or without a photograph, may be used.

Using Your Jacket
or Cover As a Direct Mail Piece

If your jacket or cover is properly prepared and printed, it should be able to sell your book, even though the prospective buyer does not have the opportunity to examine the contents. Why not have additional copies printed to be used for advertising purposes? If they are produced at the same time as the jackets or covers are printed, they are relatively inexpensive.

You can combine the jacket (or cover), with an inexpensively printed order blank (perhaps offering a special prepublication price), and mail it to friends and other potential purchasers.

You can also include the jacket, with a questionnaire card, and mail it to a selected list of newspapers and magazines, asking whether they will be interested in receiving a review copy upon publication. (If they respond, be sure to mention that they requested a copy when you forward it.) Using your jacket copy effectively is discussed further in the chapters that discuss promotion.

Paper for Jackets

A good grade of white, eighty pound coated paper, makes an attractive, durable jacket.* It will reproduce photographs, intricate artwork, and color very well.

---

*At Harlo, we normally apply a coat of press wax after printing, to jackets or covers that have been printed on gloss-finish paper. It is inexpensive and offers a satisfactory amount of protection.

Non-gloss papers with a relatively smooth finish, and non-gloss papers with a pattern embossed in the surface, are also available in white and a variety of colors.

Although this paper may be somewhat more expensive, and is perhaps not quite as wear-resistant as a coated, press-waxed sheet, the expense of press waxing can be eliminated. And, as there is a wide range of colors available, it is possible to produce an attractive jacket using only black or one color of ink.

Cover Material for Softbound Books

There are a number of materials on the market specifically manufactured for use as covers of quality softbound books. Unfortunately, in many cases the minimum order that must be placed puts them out of range of the short run book.

This does not, however, hamper the creative printer. Many sturdy cover papers, providing the grain of the paper runs the proper way, can be used for covering softbound books.

As is the case with jackets, cover material falls into two general categories: gloss finish and non-gloss finish, and the same things pertain so far as press waxing and the use of colors.

From my experience, I've found that a ten point (ten thousandths thick), white, coated one side cover, is ideal for use with illustrations and color. The application of a coat of press wax will keep the cover clean.

A sixty-five pound non-gloss finish cover stock in white or color, also works well for saddle stitched or perfect-bound books.

Special Finishes

Special, plastic-like, finishes can be applied to jackets and covers after printing. Most often, however, if the run is relatively short, the price is prohibitive. This is why I recommend press waxing.

Printing the Cover of a Hardbound Book

The covers of hardbound books can be printed in one or a number of colors. There are various materials available for use in this instance. Here, again, it is wise to bear in mind that if your run is short, the cost may be prohibitive.

7 HOW TO PREPARE AND SUBMIT ARTWORK

An interestingly illustrated jacket or cover will enhance the overall appearance and saleability of your book. If the *content* lends itself to illustration, this can be another plus.

ARTWORK SUPPLIED BY CUSTOMER

Providing you have the necessary skill, there is no reason why you cannot prepare your own artwork. Or, perhaps one of your friends will offer to do the work for you. From experience, however, I've found that working with friends can sometimes lead to embarrassing situations. It's hard to turn down something they furnish even though you feel it is not up to par. If you have doubts, employ the services of a commercial artist. Poorly executed artwork will hinder sales.

If you furnish your own artwork, be sure it has been prepared to the proper proportion. Proportion must also be taken into account when furnishing photographs, maps, and other camera-ready copy.

We produce many 5½-by-8½-inch books. Most people realize that it is practical to furnish artwork oversize, because reducing it eliminates flaws, whereas enlargement magnifies them.

So, what often happens? They submit the artwork on an 8½-by-11-inch sheet. It may sound right, but it is *wrong!* It has not been drawn to the proper proportion, because only one of the dimensions has been doubled. To have been correct, *both* measurements should have been doubled and the artwork furnished on an 11-by-17-inch sheet.

Proportion can be done *mathematically* by applying the same *percentage* of enlargement (or reduction) to *both* dimensions. Thus, if you want your finished size to be 4-by-6-inches and you increase each dimension by 50%, the artwork size should be 6-by-9-inches. If you increase each dimension by 100%, the artwork size is 8-by-12-inches. If you *decrease* each dimension by 50% the final size will be 2-by-3-inches.

Proportion can also be easily understood if you actually draw your dimensions as illustrated on the facing page. This pictorial method is a handy way to tell in advance, how photographs, or *portions* of photographs, will appear when enlarged or reduced. Remember, you need not use an entire photograph; you may decide to use only the most interesting part.

If your illustration is to bleed (run off the sheet), allow at least ⅛ inch of excess that the printer can trim off.

Before you or your artist begin preparing artwork for a cover or book jacket, get specifications from your printer. Remember, however, that he cannot tell you how much space to allow for the spine until he knows the kind of paper to be used and the actual number of pages there will be in the book.

If the final job is to be printed in more than one color, and the colors touch or overlap, the artwork should be prepared somewhat like you would make a sandwich: The dominant color should appear on the bottom sheet and the other colors on overlay sheets. You can purchase special acetate material from art supply stores for this purpose.

Any location on this line where a vertical line intersects the horizontal will be in proportion to the finished size desired.

←——Desired Finish Size

ARTWORK SUPPLIED BY PRINTER

Most printers have artists on their staff or work with capable free-lancers who are familiar with book and jacket design. The price they charge depends on the skill of the artist, the intricacy of the work, the time the artist must spend researching the subject, and the time it takes him to do the actual work.

If the artist must read your entire manuscript before he can visualize what is proper, his charge will increase. So it is wise, no matter how crude, to sketch your ideas on paper and then explain the sketch as thoroughly as possible.

If the artwork is to include a representation of a particular individual or place, send a photograph or clipping to which the artist can refer. One author, for instance, sent us a postcard depicting an historic site, along with a photograph of a landscape, and told us to combine the two in stylized form. Another person sent a newspaper clipping of the person he was featuring, together with a battlefield scene and told us to combine the two.

It is wise to request the artist to send you a sketch of what he proposes before he completes the finished art. At this point he can still incorporate your minor suggestions without a great deal of trouble. However, if you change things drastically, expect an additional charge.

The simpler you make the artist's work, the more likely he is to capture what you have in mind and the lower the cost will be.

8 PRINTING ILLUSTRATIONS IN YOUR BOOK OR ON THE JACKET

When it comes to printing, illustrations generally fall into one or two broad classifications: line illustrations and halftones.

LINE ILLUSTRATIONS

A line illustration is a drawing that is composed entirely of solid areas or lines of a single tone. A pen-and-India-ink drawing is one example; the type on this page is another. Neither contain any tones; they are solid colors.

HALFTONES

Any artwork that contains gradations of tones must be reproduced by the halftone process. Gradations are found in such original copy as photographs, paintings, and pencil drawings.

If you examine a photograph in a newspaper or maga-

zine (use a magnifying glass if necessary) you will notice
that what appears to be tones of black, is an optical illusion.

The reproduction is actually composed of thousands of
individual dots that vary in diameter in proportion to the
lightness or darkness of the tone being reproduced.

Held away from your eyes, however, the halftone looks
like a picture. The eye does not detect the dot pattern but
interprets the mixture of black ink dots and unprinted
portions of paper as tones.

The printer accomplishes this technique by photographing the original copy through a ruled screen.

Halftones need not necessarily be printed in black.
There are many special techniques for reproducing them
in color.

Two of the most common color techniques are duotones and four-color process printing.

Color Duotones

A duotone is a two-color halftone reproduction made
from a black-and-white original. Although duotones do not
have the impact of full color, their cost is much less and the
printed illustration has more depth and is considerably
more attractive than a mere black and white reproduction.

One halftone is made for the black and another for the
color. The two colors are then printed one on top of the
other.

Although we used what are called "process colors"
(cyan [process blue], magenta [process red] and yellow)
on the sample pages which follow, there are practically
unlimited color combinations. Get advice from your printer
as to which color combinations to use.

Four-color Printing

Four-color printing (process color printing) is a technique employed by printers to reproduce an infinite range
of colors with a limited number of colors of ink.

A halftone is made for the black and each of the primary colors: cyan (process blue), magenta (process red),

and yellow. When printed together they reproduce all the browns, grays, greens, oranges, purples, etc., that are in the original work.

Four-color halftones can be made directly from the artwork (a colored photograph, or painting) or, preferably, from a color transparency.

Four-color printing is relatively expensive, particularly for short runs, because the technique involves making color separations, producing four plates, and passing the paper through the press four times.

The twenty-four pages that follow show examples of typical processes for reproducing illustrations and the effect paper has on reproduction quality and color.

The first eight pages are printed on a good grade of 70# uncoated white offset paper.

The second eight pages are printed on a 60#, off-white offset paper.

The third eight pages are printed on a 70# coated (enamel finish) paper.

The same ink colors were used in each case. The printing was done by offset. Note the difference that paper makes in the final appearance.

Line drawing printed in black ink.

Line drawing printed in yellow ink.

Line Illustrations
See pages 45-48 for further explanation.
Illustrations on next eight pages courtesy
of Eastman Kodak Company.

Line drawing printed in process red.
Other colors can be used.

Line drawing printed in process blue.
Other colors can be used.

A halftone reproduced from a good original photograph. Note the contrast: white whites and black blacks.

A halftone printed in a solid color of process red ink. Other colors of ink can be used.

Halftones
Four Variations of the Same Original Photograph.
See pages 45-48 for further explanation.

An outline halftone. The background has been eliminated to emphasize the illustration.

A halftone printed in a solid color of process blue ink. Other colors can be used.

Duotones

See pages 45-48 for further explanation.

A duotone is a two-color halftone reproduction made from a black-and-white original. It is important to select a photograph that has good contrast: black blacks and white whites.

If printed in black ink, it will appear as the reproduction at the right.

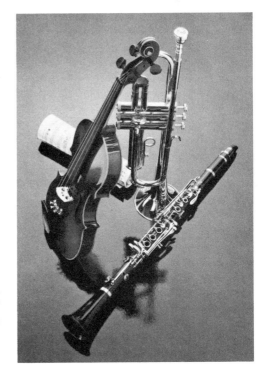

Proof of Blue printer.

Now see what happens when we add a blue halftone as shown at the right, to the black.

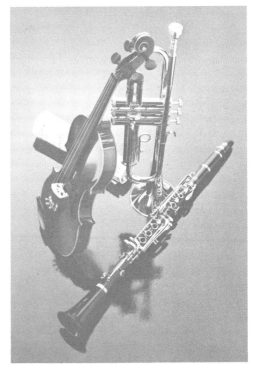

Turn page for results.

At left is shown the result of combining the black halftone with the blue halftone. The same applies when using other color combinations.

Below are examples of black and red, and black and yellow duotones, using the colors shown on the opposite page. Many other color combinations are possible.

Black and blue duotone.

Black and red duotone.

Black and yellow duotone.

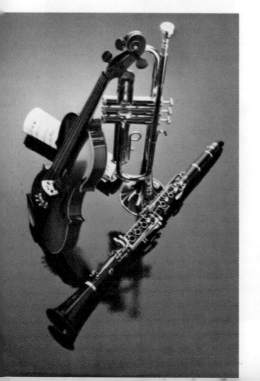

Four-Color Printing

Process
Yellow

Process
Red

Process
Blue

Process
Black

Four-color printing is a technique employed by printers to reproduce an infinite range of colors with a limited number of colors of ink.

The colors normally used—process yellow, magenta (process red), cyan (process blue) and process black—are shown above.

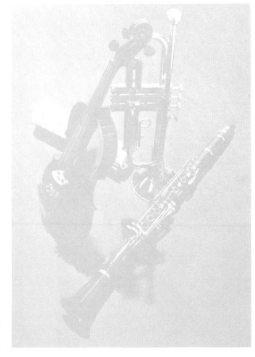

At right is shown a proof of the process yellow.

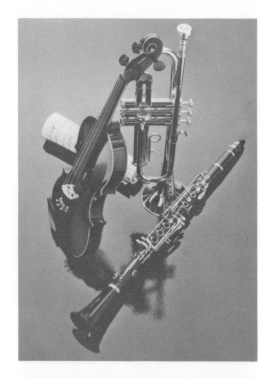

At left is shown
a proof of the
process red.

This is what happens
when the yellow and
red are combined.

At the right is shown a proof of the process blue.

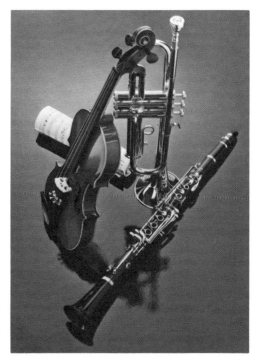

This is what happens when the yellow, red and blue are combined.

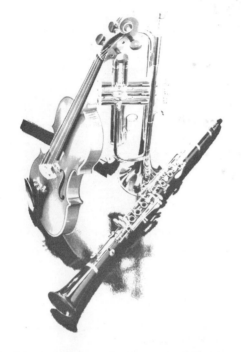

At the left is
shown a proof
of the process black.

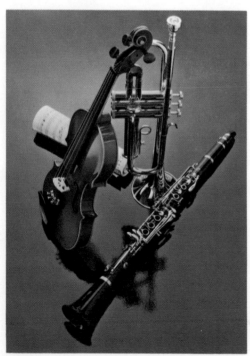

**The final result:
A combination of
the primary colors
and black.**

Line drawing printed in black ink.
Line drawing printed in yellow ink.

Line Illustrations
See pages 45-48 for further explanation.
Illustrations on next eight pages courtesy
of Eastman Kodak Company.

Line drawing printed in process red.
Other colors can be used.

Line drawing printed in process blue.
Other colors can be used.

A halftone reproduced from a good
original photograph. Note the contrast:
white whites and black blacks.

A halftone printed in a solid color
of process red ink. Other colors
of ink can be used.

Halftones
Four Variations of the Same Original Photograph.
See pages 45-48 for further explanation.

An outline halftone. The background has
been eliminated to emphasize the illustration.

A halftone printed in a solid color of
process blue ink. Other colors can be used.

Duotones

See pages 45-48 for further explanation.

A duotone is a two-color halftone reproduction made from a black-and-white original. It is important to select a photograph that has good contrast: black blacks and white whites.

If printed in black ink, it will appear as the reproduction at the right.

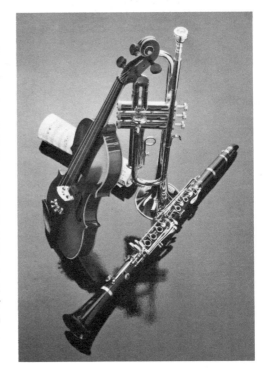

Proof of Blue printer.

Now see what happens when we add a blue halftone as shown at the right, to the black.

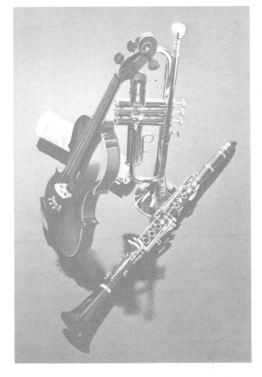

Turn page for results.

Black and blue duotone.

At left is shown the result of combining the black halftone with the blue halftone. The same applies when using other color combinations.

Below are examples of black and red, and black and yellow duotones, using the colors shown on the opposite page. Many other color combinations are possible.

Black and red duotone.

Black and yellow duotone.

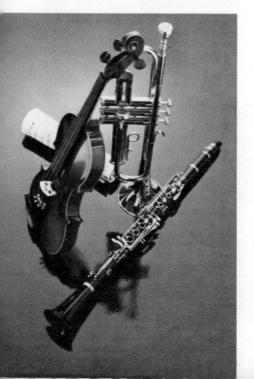

Four-Color Printing

| Process Yellow | Process Red | Process Blue | Process Black |

Four-color printing is a technique employed by printers to reproduce an infinite range of colors with a limited number of colors of ink.

The colors normally used—process yellow, magenta (process red), cyan (process blue) and process black—are shown above.

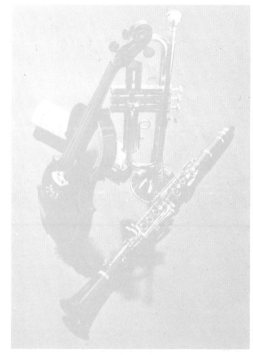

At right is shown a proof of the process yellow.

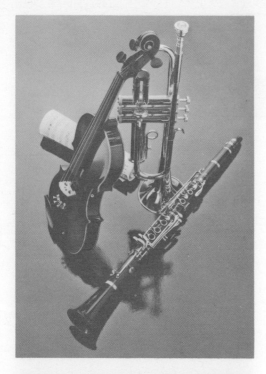

At left is shown
a proof of the
process red.

This is what happens
when the yellow and
red are combined.

At the right is
shown a proof of
the process blue.

This is what happens
when the yellow, red
and blue are combined.

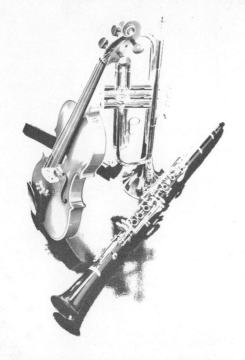

At the left is
shown a proof
of the process black.

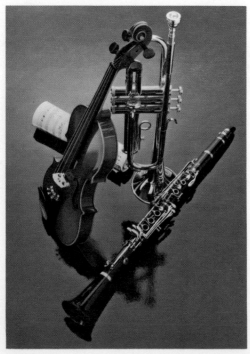

**The final result:
A combination of
the primary colors
and black.**

Line drawing printed in black ink.

Line drawing printed in yellow ink.

Line Illustrations
See pages 45-48 for further explanation.
Illustrations on next eight pages courtesy
of Eastman Kodak Company.

Line drawing printed in process red.
Other colors can be used.

Line drawing printed in process blue.
Other colors can be used.

A halftone reproduced from a good original photograph. Note the contrast: white whites and black blacks.

A halftone printed in a solid color of process red ink. Other colors of ink can be used.

Halftones
Four Variations of the Same Original Photograph.
See pages 45-48 for further explanation.

An outline halftone. The background has been eliminated to emphasize the illustration.

A halftone printed in a solid color of process blue ink. Other colors can be used.

Duotones

See pages 45-48 for further explanation.

A duotone is a two-color halftone reproduction made from a black-and-white original. It is important to select a photograph that has good contrast: black blacks and white whites.

If printed in black ink, it will appear as the reproduction at the right.

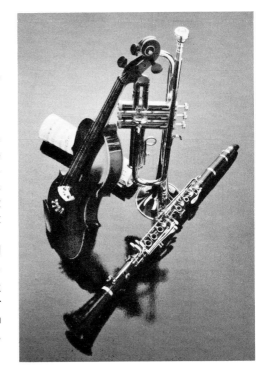

Proof of Blue printer.

Now see what happens when we add a blue halftone as shown at the right, to the black.

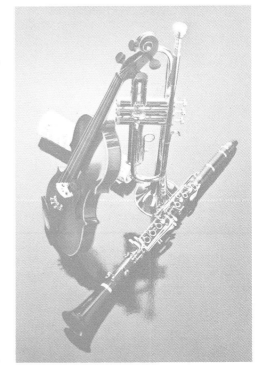

Turn page for results.

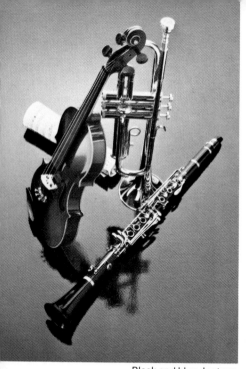

At left is shown the result of combining the black halftone with the blue halftone. The same applies when using other color combinations.

Below are examples of black and red, and black and yellow duotones, using the colors shown on the opposite page. Many other color combinations are possible.

Black and blue duotone.

Black and red duotone.

Black and yellow duotone.

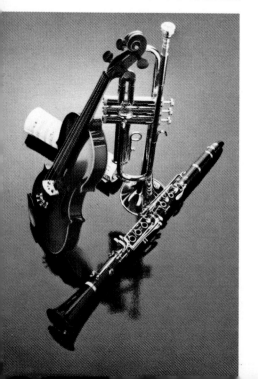

Four-Color Printing

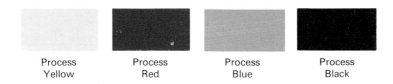

| Process Yellow | Process Red | Process Blue | Process Black |

Four-color printing is a technique employed by printers to reproduce an infinite range of colors with a limited number of colors of ink.

The colors normally used—process yellow, magenta (process red), cyan (process blue) and process black—are shown above.

At right is shown a proof of the process yellow.

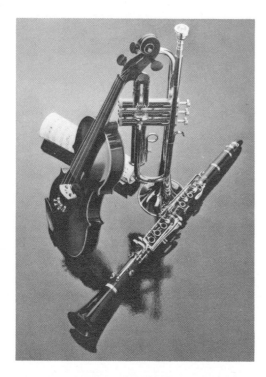

At left is shown
a proof of the
process red.

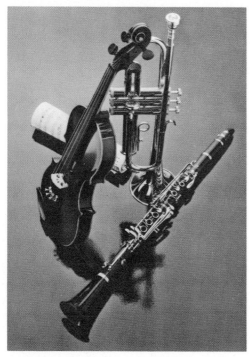

This is what happens
when the yellow and
red are combined.

At the right is
shown a proof of
the process blue.

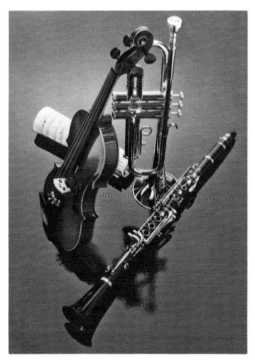

This is what happens
when the yellow, red
and blue are combined.

At the left is
shown a proof
of the process black.

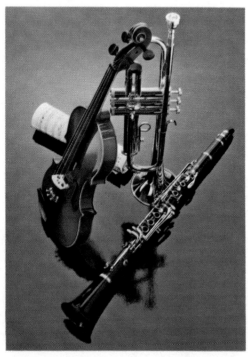

The final result:
A combination of
the primary colors
and black.

9 PROOFREADING

If your book is to be as free of errors as possible, careful proofreading is essential.

It is also one of *your* major responsibilities, because once you have read and OK'd a proof, any errors that were overlooked are no longer the printer's responsibility.

To catch errors you must train yourself to read *character by character,* instead of taking in words or phrases at a glance as you do in general reading.

I recommend that you read all proofs at least twice. If possible, have another person also read the proofs, because it is often easier to catch someone else's errors.

You will generally have two opportunities to read your copy after it has been set in type: first in galley proof form and later in page proof form.

Galley Proofs

It is virtually impossible for a worker to set type without making errors, so after the type is set, galley proofs are made. Most reliable printers will read and correct these proofs before submitting them to their customer. Some printers, and this is why you can't always rely on price alone when choosing a printer, forward the *unread* proofs directly to the customer.

Galley proofs do not reflect printing quality. They are usually furnished in strip form and contain what later will be several pages. Numbers or letters that you didn't have in your manuscript may also appear at the top of the proofs. These refer to storage areas or are the printer's instructions and will be removed by the printer later—so don't worry about them.

Even if the printer has already read and corrected the galley proofs before you receive them, there will still be typographical errors. Don't be overly concerned: Correct them. You will not be charged for errors the printer makes.

But, be exceptionally careful when you proofread galley proofs, because once you have read and OK'd them, most printers assume that everything is correct and any alterations made later will be considered *changes*—and changes are expensive.

Ideally, every manuscript should be *perfect* before it is sent to the printer. Being practical, however, this rarely happens. Somehow, when a manuscript appears in print certain things become more obvious and the author has a tendency to change them—no matter what the cost. And it can be very costly.

However, if you feel that you *must* make changes, this is the best time to make them. Your cost will be considerably less now than if you wait until the book is in page form. If changes are extensive, it is wise to request a *revised* set of galleys. Be prepared to pay extra, but get everything in order at the galley proof stage. Don't wait until the book is already in page form to make changes.

Page Proofs

After you have carefully read and returned the galley proofs, the printer will make the corrections and changes you have indicated and the book will be made into pages.

At this stage, page numbers, the contents, illustrations, captions, etc., are inserted, and everything will be on the page as it will appear when printed. If your book is to have an index, you will have to wait until you are furnished page proofs before you can insert the proper page numbers.

After he is sure everything is in proper order, the printer will make and forward a set of page proofs. As was the case with galley proofs, these do not reflect printing quality.

Read page proofs very carefully. This is the last time you will be able to check copy prior to printing.

Don't just scan to be sure errors on galley proofs were corrected. Because of mechanical problems, new errors can creep in. Be particularly careful to read entire paragraphs where words were added or deleted.

Typographical Errors

Remember that while you proofread, any deviations from the manuscript are printer's errors. These are referred to as "typographical" errors, and as they are not the fault of the author, they are corrected at the printer's expense.

Author's Alterations—Changes

Author's alterations or changes are another matter. Changes in wording, punctuation, dates, spelling—anything that deviates from the manuscript as you submitted it—are your responsibility, and the printer will normally charge for such changes at his prevailing hourly rate.

I don't know any printer who likes to make changes or who makes money (or friends) on this phase of his work. This is why it is so necessary to submit your manuscript in perfect order.

Please remember that it is necessary to reset an entire line (sometimes several lines, if the original line was "tight"), just to insert a comma. If you delete or add words at the beginning of a paragraph, the entire paragraph often must be reset.

If major changes are made in *page proofs* it may be necessary to rework the entire chapter, and perhaps change page numbers to the end of the book. So, a careful checking of the galley proofs is *absolutely essential* if there is to be no unnecessary expense on your part.

Marking Proofs

I would recommend that you use a colored pen—red is good—for marking proofs. A pencil blends too much with the color of the type.

Corrections and changes should be marked directly on the proofs, because once type is set the printer works from the proofs, not the manuscript. Most printers will ask that you indicate "OK" or "OK as corrected" on all proofs.

If it is necessary to change a large portion of copy, it is advisable to cross out the old copy on the proof and re-type the new material on a separate sheet, indicating clearly where it is to be inserted.

Editors' and Proofreaders' Marks

On the next pages are reproduced (courtesy of Dayton Typographic Service, Dayton, Ohio) a very complete set of editors' and proofreaders' marks. Proofreaders' marks are standard and most printers prefer that you use them.

Even though they are a simple way of communication, remember that *communication* is what you are after.

So if they cause you trouble, make your corrections and changes as carefully and legibly as possible . . . and unless they are involved, mark your instructions and corrections directly on the proofs, not on a separate sheet.

EDITORS'
AND PROOFREADERS' MARKS

SIZE AND STYLE OF TYPE

wf — Wrong font (size or style of type)

lc — Lower Case letter

lc — Set in LOWER CASE

c — capital letter

caps — SET IN capitals

caps + lc — Lower Case with Initial Capitals

sm. caps — SET IN small capitals

caps + s.c. — SMALL CAPITALS with initial capitals

rom — Set in roman type

ital — *Set in italic type*

L.F. — Set in lightface type

bf — **Set in boldface type**

bf ital — *Boldface italic*

Superior letter or figure[b]

Inferior letter or figure[2]

PARAGRAPHING

¶ — Begin a paragraph

no ¶ — No paragraph

run in — Run in or run on

☐ *¶* — Indent the number of em quads shown

flush — No indention

hang in — Hanging indention. This style should
have all lines after the first marked
one em — for the desired indention, either separately or by means of a bracket, as
shown

EDITORS'
AND PROOFREADERS' MARKS

INSERTION AND DELETION

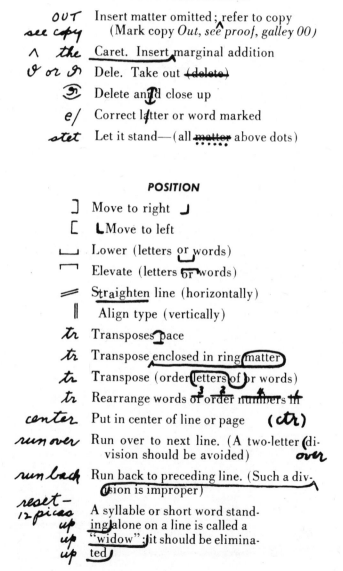

OUT   Insert matter omitted; refer to copy
see copy   (Mark copy *Out, see proof, galley 00)*

∧ the   Caret. Insert marginal addition

⸓ or ⸓   Dele. Take out (delete)

⸓   Delete and close up

e/   Correct letter or word marked

stet   Let it stand—(all matter above dots)

POSITION

]   Move to right   ⌐

[⌐Move to left

⊔   Lower (letters or words)

⊓   Elevate (letters or words)

=   Straighten line (horizontally)

‖   Align type (vertically)

tr   Transpose space

tr   Transpose enclosed in ring matter

tr   Transpose (order letters of or words)

tr   Rearrange words of order numbers in

center   Put in center of line or page   (ctr)

run over   Run over to next line. (A two-letter (division should be avoided)   over

run back   Run back to preceding line. (Such a division is improper)

reset—
12 picas   A syllable or short word stand-
up   ing alone on a line is called a
up   "widow"; it should be elimina-
up   ted)

EDITORS'
AND PROOFREADERS' MARKS

SPACING

solid Means "not leaded"

leaded Additional space between lines

⌒ Close up entirely; take out space

✳ Close up partly; leave some space

✓ *or* ⌣ Less ✓space ✓between⌣words

✕ *or* ✗ ⌗ Equalize ✓space ⌄between ✓words

hair ⌗ Hair space between letters

thin ⌗ Thin space where indicated

l/s L E T T E R - S P A C E

⌗ Insert space ⌄(or more space)

space out More ⌄space ⌄between ⌄words

en quad ½-em ⌄quad (nut) space or indention

☐ ⌄Em quad (mutton) space or indention

☐☐☐ Indent number of em quads shown

ld in⊃ Insert lead between lines

⌒ *ld* Take out lead

2 pts ⌗ Insert ⌄space ⌄(amount ⌄specified)

⌒ *1 pt* Take⌣out⌣space⌣(amount⌣specified)

PUNCTUATION

⊙ Insert period

⋏ *or* ,/ Insert comma

⊙ *or* :/ Insert colon

;/ Insert semicolon

⌄ *or* ⌄ Apostrophe or 'single quote'

⌄⌄/⌄⌄ Insert quotation marks

?/ Insert question mark

EDITORS'
AND PROOFREADERS' MARKS

!/	Insert exclamation point
-/ or =/	Insert hyphen
⊹ or /ᵉⁿ/	En dash
¹⁄ₑₘ or ⊢⊣	One-em dash
⊢²⁄ₑₘ/	Two-em dash
(/)	Insert parentheses
[/]	Insert brackets

DIACRITICAL MARKS; LIGATURES; SYMBOLS; SIGNS

ü	Diaeresis or umlaut
é	Accent acute
è	Accent grave
â	Circumflex accent or "doghouse"
ç	Cedilla or French c
ñ	Tilde (Spanish) ; til (Portuguese)
⌢	Use ligature (œ—ōeillade; ffi—affix)
⁂	Asterism .*. Leaders..........
⊙□⊙□⊙	Ellipsis____or * * * or .....
※/†/‡/	Order of symbols: *†‡§‖¶#; then double

MISCELLANEOUS

e/⊗ or ×	Replace broken or imperfect type
℘	Reverse (upside down type or cut)
⊥ or ⌄	Push down a space that prints
(SP)	Spell out (twenty gr.) *grains*
(G?)	Question of grammar
(F?)	Question of fact
2y or (?)	Query to author
(2y Ed)	Query to editor
⌐	Mark-off or break; start new line

10 HOW TO PROMOTE YOUR BOOK BEFORE IT IS PUBLISHED

Distribution (selling) is the key to success if you are publishing a book in order to make a profit. It is also the biggest problem facing the individual who publishes one book and small publishers generally.

Not that large publishers don't have problems. They know, even when applying all their expertise, that just publishing a book does not guarantee its financial success.

One large publisher told me, "Out of every ten books we publish, three lose money, four break even and three make money."

Large publishers, of course, can work on an average. You don't have this opportunity, so you have to be more careful. But you do have an advantage, because you can concentrate your efforts on one book.

No one knows all the answers to financially successful publishing. But most publishers will agree that the first requisite is *content that will interest enough prospects to purchase the book if they hear about it.*

Many books, and this does not mean the content is not good (take a history of the mushroom industry in Michigan as an example), simply do not interest enough people to make them financially successful.

This may be the main reason the manuscript was turned down by a large publisher originally.

But, after realistically examining the content of your book, let's assume that you feel enough people would buy it to make it financially successful—*if they heard about it.*

How Do You Tell Them?

By vigorously *promoting* your book *before* it is published.

By vigorously *promoting* your book *before* and *after* it is printed.

By vigorously *advertising* your book *before* and *after* it is published.

The emphasis in this chapter is on *promotion,* which in effect is a way of selling your book without spending money for actual advertising. True, many of the suggestions will take time, but when properly executed the results will be just as beneficial.

Following are some easy and inexpensive ways to assure the possibility of your book's recognition.

The sooner you start working, the greater will be your chance of success.

PRODUCE AN
ATTRACTIVE PRODUCT

Choose your printer wisely, because it is virtually impossible, no matter how good the content, to sell a book that is physically unattractive. You might be able to sell an unattractive book by direct mail, where the potential customer does not have a chance to examine it in advance, but your chances of getting it returned are also good. And if you intend to publish additional books, you are less likely to get a repeat customer. It is the repeat customer that a publisher relies on for continued success.

CHOOSE A COMPANY NAME

Although many books are produced under the printer's imprint—which has particular advantages because it gives your book a continuing address to which people may write if they wish to place an order with you, and your book was written with an aim other than financial success in mind—it is my opinion that if you wish to vigorously promote your book, it has a better chance of success if you publish it under a company name.

It doesn't make any difference if you are the author/owner, and your company is only publishing one title.

The basic, legal requirements for establishing a company name are relatively simple. Consult with your attorney. To avoid choosing a name that is already being used, carefully research such publications as *Literary Market Place* and *Writer's Market,* which list names of most publishers.

If you choose not to publish under a company name, but you still want orders to come directly to you, I'd suggest placing the retail price and your name and address on the back of the title page and on the flap of the jacket.

In either case, I'd recommend placing the printer's name and address, in small type, on the back of the title page.

OBTAINING ADVANCE COMMENTS
AND INCORPORATING THEM
WITH YOUR JACKET COPY

As an author, you undoubtedly know a number of relevant experts who will be willing to make brief comments about the contents of your book. These comments can be used effectively, not only for selling your book later, but as an aid in getting prepublication publicity.

Obtain this information as soon as possible, and then use the quotes in conjunction with your jacket or cover copy. If you haven't already done so, read the chapter on book jackets and covers.

Write and rewrite your copy until you *know* it will do a good selling job, because once properly written, you can use the same information, with slight modifications, for a number of the suggestions that follow.

You can amend and polish your wording as you go along, incorporating additional comments as you receive them.

OBTAIN A COPY OF
LITERARY MARKET PLACE

Perusing a copy of *Literary Market Place,* which is published annually by R. R. Bowker Co., 1180 Avenue of the Americas, New York, N.Y. 10036 (currently $20 but should be available in your library), will give you a veritable wealth of information and ideas. This volume lists book clubs, news services, reviewers, magazines and newspapers, major radio and television networks, book trade events, associations, mailing list suppliers and much more.

PREPUBLICATION REVIEWS

You don't have to wait until your book is printed before you start selling. Obtain as much prepublication publicity as possible. If you have the right kind of book, do your homework carefully and, I suppose have a little luck, your book could gain immediate attention.

You will need a publication date. It can be vague: "March 1977" or specific, "March 21, 1977."

Many authors assume that the day their book is completed becomes its publication date. This need not be true. Many major books go into several printings *before* the publication date.

It might be wise to set your publication date between January and July, so you will have less competition from the large publishers.

In any case, set your publication date far enough ahead to give yourself time to take advantage of the prepublication reviewing media.

There are four main sources: *Publisher's Weekly,* 1180 Avenue of the Americas, New York, N.Y. 10036 (Request an "Advance Book Information Form"); *Kirkus Reviews,*

60 West 13th Street, New York, N.Y. 10011; *Library Journal,* 1180 Avenue of the Americas, New York, N.Y. 10036; and *Forecast,* published by the Baker and Taylor Companies, 1515 Broadway, New York, N.Y. 10036.

You can send galley proofs, page proofs, photocopies (your printer can supply any of the foregoing at a moderate cost), or the bound book.

You should submit your material for review from six-to eight weeks before your publication date.

Write a covering letter to call attention to the book. Don't just send the material to the publication. Check a copy of a current issue of *Literary Market Place* and find the name of the proper person.

Tell about the book's content, your background and qualifications. Keep the letter courteous, no-nonsense. Include your telephone number, and ask the reviewer to please include the address from which books may be ordered if they review it.

If you are not sending the book, include information about the binding. Particularly stress that the book will be hardbound if this is the case.

If you do not hear anything, write another letter. It's worth the trouble. A review in any of these publications can get your book off to an excellent start. Quoting comments you receive is more likely to make other reviewers take notice and give you further publicity. A reprint of the review, along with other advertising copy that is sent to libraries or bookstores, is more likely to result in sales.

ADVANCE BOOK INFORMATION

A worthwhile free service that you should avail yourself of, if you are publishing a book under your own imprint, is to fill out an "Advance Book Information" form.

These forms are available on request from: ABI Department, R. R. Bowker Company, 1180 Avenue of the Americas, New York, N.Y. 10036.

The R. R. Bowker Company likes to receive these forms six months before your formal publication date, so they can include the information in their reference guides to American books in print. The Bowker references are used continually by professional book buyers. Remember, set your publication date far enough ahead so you can spend the intervening time promoting your book.

PREPUBLICATION ANNOUNCEMENTS TO MEDIA

Well in advance of your publication date, you should begin contacting various other media.

If your jacket or cover copy has been written in a brief, no-nonsense fashion, it can be turned into a news release by adding a few well written lead-in sentences. A sample news release appears below:

NEWS RELEASE   HARLO
                                    PRESS

16721 HAMILTON AVENUE • DETROIT, MICHIGAN 48203 • (313) UN 4-1529

For Release: Immediately
For more information call John Jones

THIRTIETH ANNIVERSARY 1976

Present your release in the form of a newspaper article. Always put the most important material in the first paragraph and then expand on this paragraph. This way, if the entire release is not printed, the story will stand by itself.

Include your photograph if you wish, but more importantly, enclose a copy of the jacket or book cover.

Make up a well thought-out mailing list. Start with your hometown papers. Add any organizational, fraternal or trade journals with which you have a connection. Don't forget church and alumni publications. Consider whether there may be an organization (historical society, church, school, group, etc.) which might place a bulk order.

HARLO PRESS

16721 HAMILTON AVENUE • DETROIT, MICHIGAN 48203 • (313) UN 4-1529

JUST PUBLISHED!

INCLUDING TWO CAPTAINS, A Later Look Westward

BY MARY PADDOCK BERTHOLD

$6.00

What was the later history of the Lewis & Clark Expedition? What became of its members after the triumphal return to St. Louis? In this, her latest book on the Northwest, Mrs. Berthold writes of Meriwether Lewis' mysterious death in the Tennessee Wilderness so soon after, in 1809. Then, as Governor of Louisiana Territory, he was on his way to Washington on official business, following the blazed trail called the Natchez Trace. She writes of Clark's successful later career as Governor of Missouri Territory and as Superintendent of Indian Affairs at St. Louis.

There were other remarkable members of this Corps of Discovery, prominent among them the three sergeants: Pryor, Ordway and Gass; the intrepid John Colter, discoverer of the Yellowstone; Lewis' favorite aide and brilliant scout, George Drouilliard; the Shoshoni Indian girl Sacajawea, who carried the youngest member of the Expedition, her infant son Baptiste, to the Pacific Ocean.

The Expedition traversed the width of Montana, from east to west and back again. Mrs. Berthold follows their route, noting the traces still evident in streams and rivers—the Great Falls of the Missouri and its headwaters at the Three Forks—the Gates of the Mountains—the Lolo Pass—the names and landmarks of the Captains' Journals.

She appends a sketch of Marcus Daly's copper town of Anaconda, where she lived for several years after her return to Montana in 1965, and noting the evidences of the Copper Baron's reign here and there about the State.

ABOUT THE AUTHOR

Mary Paddock Berthold, born in the Big Hole Basin of Southwestern Montana, attended high school in Idaho and Butte; college in Washington and Oregon. Her first job was on a Butte newspaper. She worked in radio in Toledo, Ohio, and in Missoula. After Captain Berthold's death in the South Pacific in 1943, she worked for several years in the Los Angeles office of a Lloyd's of London representative, returning to Montana in 1965 to devote her full time to writing. Her published books include the two on her home territory: TURN HERE FOR THE BIG HOLE and BIG HOLE JOURNAL, Notes and Excerpts.

Please send_____copies
INCLUDING TWO CAPTAINS, A Later Look Westward
by Mary Paddock Berthold

Name _____

Address _____

Check for _____ City & State _____ Zip _____
enclosed. Price: $6.00, plus 25¢ postage.
Order from: Mary Paddock Berthold.

Or contact: HARLO PRESS   •   16721 HAMILTON AVE.   •   DETROIT, MICHIGAN 48203

An inexpensive format that can be
used as a prepublication announcement
and later. Discussed further on next page.

Expand your list as you feel necessary. By examining a copy of *Literary Market Place,* which lists many review sources, you can build up an excellent list. When chosing magazines, try to pick a publication that will be interested in the specific content of your book.

Be selective. In many cases you will want to send a review copy of the book after it is published, so construct your list carefully. And by all means, don't overlook the publications with which you have a connection.

Pick publications interested in the subject of your book; i.e., if your book deals with history, send the release to historical publications. Finally, send it to wholesalers, large retail accounts, and the like. Be sure to enclose a reply card inviting people to request a review copy.

PREPUBLICATION SALES

Using the basic copy you prepared for your press release, add an order blank and send a mailing to friends, relatives, and any other individuals who you think will be fair prospects for purchasing your book.

Be a little "sneaky." If a person has contributed in any way to helping you write your book, or if he is mentioned in the acknowledgments, bibliography or in the text, he is a fair prospect.

If you write a book about a locality, list names. Even if the person mentioned is no longer living, his descendants will be prospects. These individuals will also mention your book to other people.

You can make the prepublication announcement sell more books by offering a special prepublication price, or by stating that all copies purchased prior to publication will be autographed.

Be sure to include the publication date—which should be *after* the books are printed. This way you can ship books prior to the publication date and avoid the confusion resulting from explaining why the book has not been sent.

You can modify this prepublication announcement slightly and continue to use it after publication.

11 HOW TO PROMOTE YOUR BOOK AFTER IT IS PUBLISHED

As in the previous chapter, the suggestions that follow rely heavily on *promotion* rather than on advertising. There is bound to be a certain amount of overlap but, generally speaking, promotion involves anything you do to make the public aware of your book without actually spending money for advertising.

Promotion, although it will take more of your time, will cost you less money. Properly done, promotion can be as valuable as advertising.

STEPS TO TAKE IMMEDIATELY AFTER YOUR BOOK COMES OFF THE PRESS

The steps which follow involve only work and complimentary copies. They may or may not result in a number of orders. At least, they will make the important media aware that your book exists.

1. Send two copies to Register of Copyrights if you are obtaining your own copyright. (Procedures are discussed in Chapter 15.)

2. If you have been preassigned a number, send one copy to Library of Congress, C.I.P. Office, Washington, D.C. 20540. (Procedures are discussed in Chapter 16.)

3. Send one copy to H. W. Wilson Co., 950 University Avenue, Bronx, N.Y. 10452, for listing in the monthly publication, *Cumulative Book Index.* Supply them the following information: Name of author, title, subject, edition, size of book, number of pages, number of illustrations, kind of binding, retail price, date of publication, name and address from which book can be ordered. There is no charge.

4. Send one copy to "Weekly Record" of *Publisher's Weekly,* 1180 Avenue of the Americas, New York, N.Y. 10036. There is no charge for this service. A listing in the "Weekly Record" is not a recommendation on the part of *Publisher's Weekly.* It is a notification that the book exists. Books must contain forty-nine or more pages.

5. If your book is the kind that libraries might order, send a review copy to *Library Journal,* 1180 Avenue of the Americas, New York, N.Y. 10036. A review, or even a mention, in this publication will result in orders.

6. If your book has general appeal, it might be wise to send a complimentary copy to a few large book jobbers who might list it in their catalogs. Three such companies are:
   Academic Library Services, Baker & Taylor Co., 6 Kirby Avenue, Somerville, N.J. 08876
   American Library Association, 50 East Huron Street, Chicago, Ill. 60611
   Bro-Dart Books, Inc., Box 921, Williamsport, Pa. 17701

7. Don't overlook the almost free advertising resulting from a listing in three important publications produced by R. R. Bowker Co., 1180 Avenue of the Americas, New

York, N.Y. 10036: *Books in Print, Publishers Trade List Annual* and *Subject Guide to Books.*

Contact Bowker before sending your book to obtain rates and other information.

Generally you will be asked to supply the following information: Title, name of author, year of publication, number of pages, number of illustrations, kind of binding, retail price, subject and table of contents, name and address of person or publisher from whom book may be ordered. *Books in Print,* no matter what the subject of your book, will let some people know that your book exists who otherwise would not have known. This publication also accepts advertisements of various sizes and will be happy to supply rates.

SENDING REVIEW COPIES

Simply by calling attention to your book, regardless of what he says, a reviewer can influence thousands of book-oriented consumers.

It is perhaps the biggest bargain that you can get if you are on a limited budget, because all it costs is time, review copies and postage.

But, remember that you have to live by the rules. Review copies should be mailed well in advance (six-to-eight weeks) of your publication date. Many publications will not review books *after* the publication date.

If you sent a prepublication announcement, your top priority should be the people who responded to the announcement. When you contact them, be sure to mention that they requested a review copy.

But, even if you failed to send a prepublication release, you can still send review copies.

Smaller newspapers and magazines often do not have the staff or time to write a critical review, so write one yourself and include it with the book.

Don't be too modest. After all, your book is *good.* Tell why it's good. Also tell about yourself, because you are an integral part of your book.

From experience, I've found that many reviewers either quote directly or paraphrase a well written press release or jacket copy, so write what you want repeated. If you've already had some reviews, send copies to lend credence to your release.

PICK YOUR PUBLICATION CAREFULLY

There are hundreds of possible sources. Pick and choose carefully. If your book is about an area, pick a publication in that area. If your book is about a particular subject, pick publications interested in the subject. Of course, always include your local papers, alumni magazines, trade journals, etc.

The *Ayer Directory of Publications,* which should be available in your library, lists and describes all magazines and newspapers published in the U.S. and Canada. *Literary Market Place* also lists major book reviewers.

SAMPLE
OF BOOK
REVIEW
SLIP

HARLO PRESS
Presents for Review . . .

TITLE How To Publish Your Own Book
AUTHOR L.W. Mueller
PUBLICATION DATE August 1, 1976
PRICE $4.95 Softbound)
$7.95 Hardbound)

We will appreciate receiving two copies of any review that appears.

HARLO PRESS
16721 HAMILTON AVENUE
DETROIT, MICHIGAN 48203

It's also a good idea to enclose a review slip (see illustration) or stamp the publication date and price on the title page or inside cover.

You can branch out after taking care of your priority list as broadly as you wish. But, be selective. Don't mail unless you think you have at least a fair chance of getting a review.

Don't worry if you get a bad review. People remember titles more than they do reviews.

RADIO AND TELEVISION

It is easier than many people think to appear on local radio and television—particularly the talk shows.

I would suggest writing a formal letter on your own behalf. Include a copy of your book, a press release and copies of any reviews you have received. Also include your telephone number. But just as important, tell the station about yourself and why your book is unique.

If you are not contacted, follow up your letter with a phone call. Be prepared to be shunted around. Don't lose your temper!

It costs practically nothing to try. You have everything to gain.

TRY FOR A FEATURE STORY

Even though people buy books because of their content, they are equally as interested in the author.

A feature story about you in your local paper, trade organization magazine, or alumni publication, will have as beneficial an effect as though your book is reviewed.

The author of *Honeymoon in a Taxicab,* which is currently in its sixth printing, is a master of this technique.

Newspapers have featured him several times a year for a number of years—not always about his book, although the articles carried a plug.

He recently appeared on television discussing "No Fault Insurance." The jacket of his book, although the subject was far removed, was displayed on the screen. A few years ago he appeared on television on New Year's Eve.

The fact that he is an author is what makes him the expert. If reporters want to know what is happening in the cab business in Detroit, it's gotten so they automatically think of him as an authority. He is, but so are a lot of other cab drivers. He, however, is an author.

Don't be bashful. Be enthusiastic! Energetic! Sell yourself! You will also sell your book.

SET UP SPEAKING ENGAGEMENTS

Word-of-mouth advertising may be slow, but it is sure. It costs only time and postage to inform local service organizations and chambers of commerce, PTA's, library associations and book and author organizations, adult education programs, church-and-school-affiliated organizations, that you are available as a speaker. If you speak to one group you are likely to be invited to speak to another. Grassroots promotion? Sure! But it's worth it.

Some of Harlo's most successful authors have relied heavily on speaking engagements to sell their books. I'm reminded of one author who wrote a volume of down to earth, family type, good-sense poetry. Everyone knows this type of poetry doesn't sell. But his did! He lectured, and sold books while doing so, to Grange groups. His book went into several printings.

AUTOGRAPH PARTIES

If you are somewhat of a personality in your community, and particularly if your book has either wide sales appeal or is slanted toward your area of the country, you might be able to persuade a local book store to sponsor an autograph party. Naturally the event must be advertised or no one will come. The book store might be more receptive if you underwrite at least part of the cost. Of course you should also do your own bit by calling or sending a mailing to friends and other people who might attend.

WRITE ARTICLES FOR
NEWSPAPERS OR MAGAZINES

The fact that you are a published author will open doors that have been closed to you before. You may be more well known for the daily job you do than for your book. But, you can always slip in the fact (or the publication may do it) that you are the author of so and so.

SELLING SUBSIDIARY RIGHTS

Subsidiary rights, which in effect is giving someone else the permission to reproduce or use your material, is an aspect of publishing that individuals rarely actively pursue. But it could result in an unexpected windfall.

The content of your book will determine whether you should pursue this avenue of promotion.

The possibilities, however, are unlimited. They can encompass every aspect from book club rights to mass paperback rights, from foreign translation rights to magazine excerpting rights, from newspaper and other periodical installments to film rights, on down to permission to reprint in anthologies, which has occurred with many of the authors for whom we have produced books.

If this aspect interests you, and you haven't already done so, obtain a copy of *Literary Market Place*. This publication lists names and addresses that offer unlimited possibilities.

But be careful to pick your prospect carefully. A book club dealing with history is not interested in a cook book.

If your book lends itself to excerpting in newspapers or magazines, even though the payment may be moderate, don't overlook this outlet, as the advertising value could be worth more than any monetary reward you receive.

Subsidiary rights are more likely to boost sales than detract from them.

You don't have to wait until a book is published before contacting prospects. Many large publishers sell subsidiary rights well in advance of publication by using galley or page proofs.

Be frank. Tell your prospects what you have in mind and that you will cooperate in any way you can. Back up your letter with copies of reviews and any other sales ammunition you can muster.

JOINING
PROFESSIONAL ORGANIZATIONS

If you are really serious about publishing, there are a number of organizations that can offer help in a variety of manners.

If you are only publishing one book, the cost of belonging may not be practical because membership fees are high.

Any of the following will be glad to give you additional information:

American Booksellers Association
800 Second Avenue
New York, N.Y. 10017

The American Library Association
50 East Huron Street
Chicago, Ill. 60611

The Association of American Publishers, Inc.
1 Park Avenue
New York, N.Y. 10016

The Association of American University Presses
1 Park Avenue
New York, N.Y. 10016

The Christian Booksellers Association
2031 West Cheyenne Road
Colorado Springs, Colo. 80906

The National Association of College Stores
528 East Lorain Street
Oberlin, Ohio 44074

12 HOW TO SELL YOUR BOOK AFTER IT IS PRINTED

The two preceding chapters dealt primarily with promotion. You'll remember that I defined promotion as any way of selling your book other than actual advertising.

As mentioned, there obviously is a certain amount of overlap, but this chapter will deal primarily with methods of selling your book *other* than promotion.

Generally this will involve itself with advertising and will call for a larger outlay of money. This doesn't necessarily mean that it need be expensive. If your advertising produces results, it will be inexpensive.

The various suggestions for selling that follow, all presuppose that your book has sales potential to one degree or another. Pick what you consider practical in your case.

SELLING THROUGH BOOK JOBBERS

Don't overlook book jobbers, as they can offer a steady outlet for your book. Because they resell the books they order, they normally like to work on at least a forty percent discount. Jobbers generally pay their bills promptly (which isn't always the case with bookstores), and they may place standing orders which will simplify your bookkeeping. Because of the paperwork involved, I'd only give a twenty percent courtesy discount for individual orders.

Jobbers normally do not deal in promotion, which is still up to you. Their main customers are libraries. A library may give the jobber a long list of books from a number of publishers and let him fill the orders. This is convenient for the library because the jobber does all ordering and the library pays only one bill. *Literary Market Place* lists book jobbers, together with their specialties.

SELLING TO CHAIN BOOKSTORES

Sales to chain bookstores, providing your book has enough general appeal to interest them, offer a significant potential outlet. Even though they will want a substantial discount (at least forty percent), remember that they buy for a number of stores. Their credit is generally good and they will pay more promptly than many of the individual stores. You must take the initiative. It is unlikely that they will contact you.

I would say that sending a complimentary examination copy (you can stamp it "complimentary" if you wish), together with a covering letter and reproductions of any reviews you have received, will be worth trying.

Bowker's *American Book Trade Directory* has a complete list of main-office buyers for chains. Following are some of the larger chain bookstores.

> Doubleday Book Shops
> 673 Fifth Avenue
> New York, N.Y. 10022

> Dayton-Hudson
> (Buys for Pickwick stores and B. Dalton)
> 9340 James Avenue South
> Minneapolis, Minn. 55431

Cokesbury
201 Eighth Avenue South
Nashville, Tenn. 37203

Brentano's
6 West 48th Street
New York, N.Y. 10017

Walden Book Company, Inc.
179 Ludlow Street
Stamford, Conn. 06904

CALL ON BOOKSTORES, JOBBERS AND CHAIN BOOKSTORE BUYERS PERSONALLY

Nothing beats personal contact. There is no reason why, if you have a saleable book, you can't contact bookstores, jobbers or chain bookstore buyers personally.

These outlets may be in your locality or you might want to make a few calls while traveling elsewhere. In order to save time, phone ahead for an appointment.

Be courteous. Bring a copy of your book, along with copies of any reviews you may have received.

Be Prepared

Your prospective client is more interested in making money than he is in helping you.

Point out why your book is unique and why it will sell if properly displayed.

Thoroughly familiarize yourself with normal discount and return procedures. These items are discussed in Chapter 13.

Have some type of an order blank handy, and don't forget to ask for a purchase order number if your client requires one, and for routing instructions that should appear on the shipping label.

Although in some cases it might work, I don't recommend leaving books on a consignment basis unless the store is located close enough so you can personally check back.

Follow Up Your Sales

Once sold, follow up to see whether additional books are needed. It might be wise to send a personal note, together with an order blank, every month or two.

CO-OP DIRECT MAIL ADVERTISING

The cost of printing, postage and mailing to a large list of names may be prohibitive if you are advertising only one book.

There are, however, a number of companies who will combine your advertising with that of other publishers and mail to selected lists: libraries, bookstores, people who buy books through the mail.

One such company is Quick Card Info Service for Libraries, 211 East 43rd Street, New York, N.Y. 10017.

As their method of operation, the market they reach and costs vary, I would suggest you contact co-op mailers *before* planning your mailing piece.

If your results are worthwhile, a mailing to the same list in four- to six-week intervals should bring practically the same results.

From your standpoint, you will also find this method of direct mail is quite simple. The companies will give you specifications for the mailing piece. In some cases all you need do is supply copy. They will do the printing. I would, however, recommend that you supply camera-ready artwork, so your advertising piece turns out the way you want it to. In some cases you will have to furnish printed advertising.

In all cases they handle all details of furnishing the mailing list, addressing, postage, and mailing. The orders come back to you. Be sure to key your order blanks with a letter or number so you know what results you obtain.

COMMISSION SALESMEN

Large commercial publishers generally have their own sales force whose main job is to call on bookstores in order to familiarize them with upcoming titles, take orders, and generally service the account. The sales in the bookstore are generated mainly by the promotion and advertising the publisher does.

If you have only one book to sell, you naturally can't afford to call on all stores. One possible way of contact is through commission salesmen who handle the books of a number of publishers.

Publisher's Weekly carries a classified ad section, one heading of which is "Sales Representation." A typical ad might read: "Lines wanted immediately for exclusive distribution to libraries, schools and retail accounts. Commission pro ready to serve you. Can guarantee results."

The big "if" is whether your book has enough appeal. Checking through current and back issues of this publication will give you a list well worth contacting.

Remember that a commission salesman, as the title implies, works on a commission and will generally want a percentage of the gross generated in his area—whether the sales were a direct result of his work or your own promotion and advertising.

ATTENDING EXHIBITS

Large publishers may be able to afford to treat the display of their books at exhibits as *promotion*. But, if you are the author of a single book or a small publisher, you will be wise to treat it as *advertising* and not invest money unless you have a reasonable expectation of sufficient sales to pay the freight.

As a matter of interest, I'll list the sponsors of the four major exhibits. You can contact them if you would like additional information, although costs may be prohibitive.

The American Booksellers Association
800 Second Avenue
New York, N.Y. 10017

The American Library Association
50 East Huron Street
Chicago, Ill. 60611

The National Association of College Stores
528 East Lorain Street
Oberlin, Ohio 44074

The Christian Booksellers Association
2031 West Cheyenne Road
Colorado Springs, Colo. 80906

But, by wisely using the specialties offered by several exhibiting services, which jointly display the books of a number of publishers, you have a chance to display your book rather economically.

The fees are generally computed on a per book basis and you need not attend the exhibit personally. If you wish additional information, contact any of the organizations which follow:

Books on Exhibit, Inc.
North Bedford Road
Mount Kisco, N.Y. 10549

College Marketing Group, Inc.
198 Ash Street
Reading, Maine 01867

The Conference Book Service, Inc.
705 Prince Street
Alexandria, Va. 22314

The Combined Book Exhibit, Inc.
Scarborough Park
Albany Post Road
Briarcliff Manor, N.Y. 10510

DIRECT MAIL ADVERTISING

As about one-fourth of all books purchased each year are purchased as a result of mail order promotion, direct mail offers perhaps the greatest potential for the small publisher or the author of an individual book.

The content of the book, the actual sales pitch you make, the attractiveness and uniqueness of your mailer, and *very importantly,* the list you mail to, will determine whether you succeed or fail.

If you did the homework suggested in the two previous chapters, you should already have fairly good advertising copy.

The simplest mailer will be a modification of the promotional mailer you sent earlier. The most effective mailing list should also be the one you have prepared earlier.

If you want to expand your mailing, it may be wise to prepare a more professional mailing piece. Taken as part of the overall cost (postage, mailing, cost of list) the layout and printing is a minor portion.

You may wish to consult an advertising agency or at least a layout man to help you.

But remember this: If you don't sell your prospective buyer in the first few seconds, more than likely your mailing piece will wind up in the waste basket.

How Do You Get the
Prospective Buyer's Immediate Attention?

You get the prospective buyer's immediate attention through the use of a few choice words or an illustration that lets the prospect know, *right off,* that this book is relevant and unique—*to him!* This "teaser" copy should also be suggestive enough so that he will want to read further.

It can appear on the outside of an envelope (*making* the prospect open the envelope), or on the address side of a self-mailer (*making* him open and read on). Repeating the statement again on the inside gives double impact, as well as telling him where to start reading.

The rest of the copy should highlight important aspects of the book (remember a prospective purchaser is more likely to believe a reviewer's comments or a testimonial than your own comments) and lead him automatically to the order blank—which to you is the important item.

The order blank must be explicit. It should repeat the price, discount (if any), terms, sales tax (if applicable), whether shipping costs are included or are extra, deadline for taking advantage of a special offer. Guaranteeing to refund money if the customer is not satisfied, is also important. The customer must, of course, return the book in good condition within the time span you specify.

Make the order blank as easy to detach and use as possible.

By all means code your order blank, so you know where orders come from. To save money when printing, I'd suggest that you start with a relatively long code number, say "Dept. 1234." If you want to change codes to reflect a different mailing, have the printer stop the press and delete the last digit.

Where Do I Get Mailing Lists?

If you plan a modest mailing you can make up your own list by consulting the numerous directories which are available.

There are about 9,000 public libraries, 3,000 college libraries, 17,000 public high school libraries, 43,000 elementary school libraries and 6,000 general bookstores in this country.

If you wish to contact these areas, two excellent services are:

> R. R. Bowker Co.
> Attn: Mr. Sal Vicidomini
> 1180 Avenue of the Americas
> New York, N.Y. 10036
> Phone (212) 764-5223

> American Library Association
> Attn: Mr. Robert Hershman
> 50 East Huron Street
> Chicago, Ill. 60611

You can also obtain a list of university press book buyers from The Educational Directory, 1 Park Avenue, New York, N.Y. 10016.

Direct Mail Lists Rates and Data, published by Standard Rate and Data Service, 5201 Old Orchard Road,

Skokie, Ill. 60076, details many sources other than libraries and bookstores.

Most rental lists are zip coded on computer printout forms so they can be readily and inexpensively affixed to your mailing piece, easily bundled, and made ready for mailing under bulk rate.

You need not rent entire lists. Bowker and the American Library Association, as well as other organizations, will rent you *selective* lists which break down libraries, for instance, by the size of their book buying appropriations and bookstores by their specialities: general, religious, metaphysical, black studies.

One time use of the lists generally costs from $25 to $35 per 1000 names. Charges and specifications vary according to the list, but you can obtain free information and study what is available prior to placing your order.

Unless you have money to burn, test first. You can tell whether a mailing list is going to pay off by mailing to a portion of the list. Let the response you received (you can tell if your order blank was keyed) be the determining factor. Don't let your emotions rule.

From experience I would state that libraries, even though the orders you receive will be smaller (and some may eventually come through jobbers rather than the library itself), offer more potential than bookstores. Credit problems are also practically non-existant. The content of your book, of course, will also have a bearing.

SPACE ADVERTISING

Advertising your book in a newspaper or other periodical may seem, at first glance, the easiest possible way to sell your book. All you have to do is place an ad and wait for the orders to roll in.

It doesn't, however, always work this way. Space advertising has to be approached very carefully. If not, it is likely that you won't even get enough money back to pay for the ad—not counting the labor and cost of the book. It's true; so be cautious.

Just because you see so many book ads, don't be mislead. Large publishers often place ads for reasons other than selling an individual book.

Often they are supporting bookstores. This is very unlikely to work in your case, because your book will not be available in enough stores.

Sometimes they run ads to help build up a suitable mailing list in order to sell similar books later by direct mail. Unless you intend to publish more books in the same subject category, this method of advertising will be worthless to you.

At other times they will place ads which help serve as door openers for their salesmen. This, again, is not for you.

You have to generate enough sales from your ad to make it practical. This won't be easy because you will be competing with large publishers and book clubs which list a large number of books—often at a discount.

Some books, though, do lend themselves to space advertising—providing the ad is carefully prepared, placed in the right publication, and the cost to selling price ratio is significant. The retail price should also be high enough to warrant filling orders.

If I haven't discouraged you so far, here are a few hints.

Study Your Potential Market

Analyze very carefully the kind of person who is a prospective purchaser of your book. This is, perhaps, the single most important thing to consider.

An ad in your hometown paper, if your book is about bottle collecting, isn't likely to pull any significant response. It could, perhaps, get *you* some publicity, but advertising in a publication that goes to persons interested in your *subject* will be more worthwhile.

Cost, Deadlines, Specifications

Write to the publications which sound promising and ask for a rate card. This card will break down the costs, give circulation data, stipulate how copy should be furnished, and give you deadlines for submitting copy. The deadline for submitting copy may be several months prior to publication. If you are not thoroughly familiar with the publication, request a sample copy.

Standard Rate and Data lists most publications, together with addresses, general circulation and rates.

Space Advertising
Is Expensive

A full-page ad in the prestigeous *New York Times Sunday Book Review* section costs over $4,000. So, proceed cautiously.

Check the rates of various applicable publications and pick out the one or two that sound most practical to you. Don't go overboard! You can always branch out.

Prepare Your Copy and Artwork Carefully

Your ad has to be prepared properly. The copy should come right to the point. You must capture the reader's attention *immediately,* through the use of a few well chosen words or proper artwork.

After you've gotten his attention you must keep him interested and, finally, you must make it very clear what you want the reader to do: buy your book!

Your ad has to stand out on the page. Unless you expect to repeat the ad over and over, it should be large enough to command attention.

I would not simply send my copy to a periodical and have them set it up any way they want. I would prepare a very comprehensive layout or, better still, furnish them with camera-ready artwork.

You can enlist the aid of an advertising agency (don't contact the larger ones unless you have a big budget) to place your ad. Advertising agencies receive a commission from the periodical, so the cost for the *space* will not cost you more. They will, however, charge extra for artwork or any other services they perform.

Be Sure to Add an
Order Blank and Key Your Ad

The only way you can tell if an ad is paying its way is by keying it. Keep track of your responses. If the ad doesn't pay, drop it like a hot potato and try another publication. If it works, keep trying it until it peters out. Be hard headed; don't advertise unless it pays off.

13 DISCOUNTS AND RETURN PRIVILEGES

A single book purchased by an individual is usually sold at full retail price. Payment should accompany the order. Unless otherwise stipulated on your order blank, you pay the postage.

DISCOUNTS TO WHOLESALERS, BOOKSTORES, SCHOOLS, AND LIBRARIES

Wholesalers and bookstores normally receive a discount on books they order. Traditionally, this is in the neighborhood of forty percent for bookstores, fifty percent for wholesalers.

To encourage schools and libraries to order directly from the publisher, instead of the wholesaler with his larger discount, they are often allowed a twenty percent discount.

If you give a discount to anyone, the shipping cost is added to the invoice.

It takes nearly as long and costs practically as much to fill a small order as a large one. As a result, I would recommend the following discount schedule:

1- 4 books	20%
5-24 books	40%
25-49 books	43%
50-99 books	46%
100 or more books	50%

To keep things from getting complicated, I would adopt a single discount schedule based on the number of copies ordered, giving wholesalers and bookstores the same discount. If a wholesaler wants a larger discount, he can obtain it by ordering more books.

In my opinion, giving discounts to schools and libraries is not necessary. Any sales you lose as a result of selling at full price, generally will be more than compensated by the extra money you receive.

If you do decide to give libraries and schools a discount, do not give it unless they order five or more books.

You do not have to follow the discount schedule I recommend. But, whatever discounts you decide to give, adopt a firm policy.

TERMS

You will also have to adopt a policy in regard to terms. Bookstores and wholesalers should pay your invoice within thirty days. If they don't, they should not be allowed a discount. And I would stipulate this on the invoice: "No discount allowed unless paid by such and such a date."

Even this will not result in payment in all cases. What then? Wait a few more days and write a polite note stating, "No doubt you overlooked the terms indicated on our invoice 7691512. We appreciate your patronage and will thus extend the deadline by ten days, at which time we will expect your check."

If you do not receive payment within a reasonable time, send an invoice based on the *list* price of the book, along with a copy of your return policies. It's better to have the books returned, even though they were not sold, than to have your client keep the books and still not pay.

Single Copy Order Plan (SCOP)

You will, perhaps, receive some small orders that include a check, which has arbitrarily deducted one-third of the retail price. What should you do? I'd say fill the order. It will cost you more to inform a bookstore that your discount is twenty percent than you will lose.

Also, some companies may send you a blank check (restricted to a certain top amount) with their order. Great! Fill in the check, giving your normal discount, minus postage, type your invoice and mark it "Paid," and ship the books promptly.

RETURN PRIVILEGES

Now comes the rough part: returns. Although it may seem a lousy way to do business, wholesalers and bookstores will expect that they have the right to return unsold books. There is, however, a redeeming factor: If they didn't have this privilege, they would be less likely to try to market your books.

There are many policies in effect. Some publishers require stores to send a "Request to Return" before they will accept copies. The time limits within which various publishers will accept returns, also varies.

In the interest of simplicity, I would suggest that you adopt a policy somewhat as follows:

> *Return Policy:* Books in saleable condition may be returned for credit not less than 90 days, nor more than 12 months, after date of publisher's invoice. If books are returned with a copy of the invoice 100% of the invoice price, minus postage, will be credited; otherwise, it will be assumed that the original discount was 50%.

Your customer is obligated to pay the postage for returns.

Because bookstores are dealing with them on a continuing basis, large publishers usually issue credit rather than sending a check. If you are a small publisher or the publisher of a single book, I would mail the refund promptly. The word gets around pretty fast if you don't meet your obligations.

Your discount and return privilege policies should be committed to writing and become a part of all appropriate order forms. You can also rubber stamp this information directly on your invoice.

14 INVOICING AND SHIPPING

Although there are firms that specialize in book storage, mailing and shipping (consult *Literary Market Place*), most authors and small publishers perform these tasks themselves. They are not complicated or costly.

Don't let orders pile up. Ship and invoice them promptly. After all, sales are what you have been waiting for. The more rapidly you process orders, the sooner you will receive your money. Speedy shipping also builds good will.

INVOICING

On the following page is illustrated the first part of a multiple-copy, carbon-interleaved invoice that we have developed for our own use. One typing takes care of everything: invoice, shipper (or packing slip), shipping label, and the necessary control copies.

If you are invoicing only a few books, you may not want to go to the expense of printing quite so elaborate a

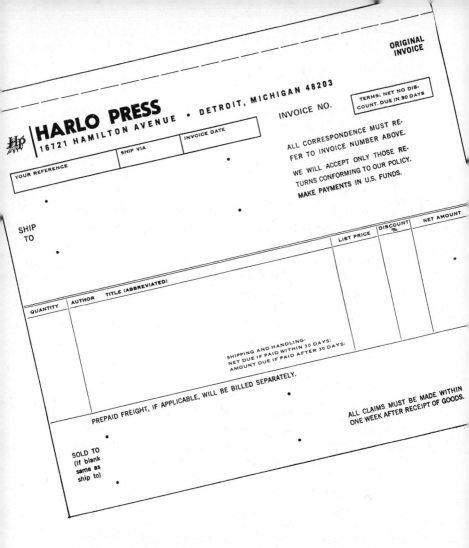

form. Standard invoices that you can adapt for your own use are available at most office supply stores, either as single copies or already carbon-interleaved. If you have the time, you can also type the entire invoice.

Regardless of how you proceed, your invoice should have the following information:

1. Date.

2. Invoice number. (You can pre-number your invoices or you might consider having your invoice number reflect the year, month, day and time the order was processed—7691512 [1976, 9th month, 15th day, at 12 o'clock].

Using this system, you can readily tell when invoices are due and whether returns are being made within required time limits.)

3. Customer Purchase Order Number. (This number, sometimes called a "P.O. Number," will appear on your *customer's* purchase order. It must be indicated on your invoice, because this is the number your customer refers to when he is checking incoming orders, routing his books, and processing payments.)

4. Shipping address.
5. Billing address if different from shipping address.
6. Quantity of books shipped.
7. Title and author.
8. List price.
9. Discount.
10. Net price.
11. Shipping charges.
12. Net if paid within 30 days.
13. Amount due if paid after 30 days.

On the next page is shown another part of the carbon-interleaved form previously illustrated. It contains the shipper (or packing slip) and a detachable label.

The Shipper or Packing Slip

Unless you include your invoice with the book, which you can't always do, because sometimes you will be requested to ship books to one address and the invoice to another, you will have to include a shipper. Your customer needs this in order to check incoming orders against his purchase order. With the exception of prices, discount, terms and shipping charges, your shipper should have the same information as your invoice.

Labels and Postage

You will also need a label. Stock shipping labels are available at office supply stores. However, in order to take advantage of the special postage rate for books, somewhere

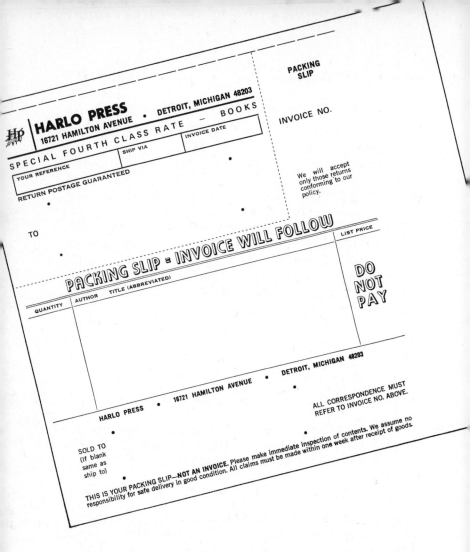

PACKING
SLIP

INVOICE NO.

We will accept
only those returns
conforming to our
policy.

HARLO PRESS • DETROIT, MICHIGAN 48203
16721 HAMILTON AVENUE — BOOKS

SPECIAL FOURTH CLASS RATE

INVOICE DATE

SHIP VIA

YOUR REFERENCE

RETURN POSTAGE GUARANTEED

TO

LIST PRICE

PACKING SLIP = INVOICE WILL FOLLOW

DO
NOT
PAY

QUANTITY   AUTHOR   TITLE (ABBREVIATED)

DETROIT, MICHIGAN 48203

16721 HAMILTON AVENUE

ALL CORRESPONDENCE MUST
REFER TO INVOICE NO. ABOVE.

HARLO PRESS

SOLD TO
(If blank
same as
ship to)

THIS IS YOUR PACKING SLIP—NOT AN INVOICE. Please make immediate inspection of contents. We assume no
responsibility for safe delivery in good condition. All claims must be made within one week after receipt of goods.

on the label or face of the package you must indicate:
"Special Fourth Class Rate—Books." If your stock label
has other wording, trim it off or cross it out.

The current rate for shipping books to any location in
the fifty-one states is twenty-one cents for the first pound
and nine cents for each additional pound.

There are also special rates for mailing to foreign
countries, but there are also regulations. Rates change, so
whether you are mailing here or abroad, check with your
post office for current rates and regulations.

SHIPPING

Thin, saddle stitched books, can be mailed in a sturdy, twenty-eight pound, clasp envelope. Be sure the envelope is large enough so the edges allow protection to the contents.

If the order is for one or two copies, clothbound and perfect-bound books can be mailed in a padded shipping bag.

Small quantities of clasp envelopes and padded shipping bags are available at most office supply stores. If you need larger quantities, check with your book printer or local printers' supply house.

Large orders of books should be shipped in the proper size corrugated carton. Check your local *Yellow Pages* for suppliers, or cut down larger boxes that you may have on hand.

15 COPYRIGHT LAW AS IT PERTAINS TO BOOKS

Our Constitution (Article 1, Section 8) states "The Congress shall have the Power . . . To promote the Progress of Science and useful Arts, by securing for limited Times to Authors and Inventors the exclusive Right to their respective Writings and Discoveries."

Under the U.S. Copyright Law (Title 17 of the U.S. Code) the owner of a copyright is granted by law certain exclusive rights. These include:

the right to print, reprint, and copy the work.

the right to sell or distribute copies of the work.

the right to transform or revise the work by means of dramatization, translation, musical arrangement, or the like.

the right to record the work.

NOTE: It is the act of publication with notice that actually secures copyright protection. If copies are published without required notice, the right to secure copyright is lost and cannot be restored.

Your copyright not only adds prestige to your material but it protects it from being reprinted without your permission.

Who Can Claim a Copyright?

Only the author or those deriving their rights through him can rightfully claim copyright. Mere ownership of a manuscript, painting, or other material does not necessarily give the owner the right to copyright. In the case of works made for hire, it is generally the employer, and not the employee, who is regarded as the author.

Minors may claim copyright; however, state laws may regulate or control the conduct of business dealings involving copyrights owned by minors.

What Can be Copyrighted?

The copyright law lists 14 broad classifications, one of which is books. Books cover such things as "published works of fiction and nonfiction, poems, compilations, composite works, directories, catalogs, annual publications, information in tabular form, and similar text matter, with or without illustrations, that appear as a book, pamphlet, leaflet, card, single page, or the like."

Copyright pertains to the content of the book. Titles, except in special circumstances where they may be subject to protection under the trademark law, cannot be copyrighted. The test of whether material is covered by copyright law, rests in its originality.

What Cannot be Copyrighted?

Even though most original work can be protected by copyright, there are several categories of material that are not eligible for copyright protection. Among others, these include:

- titles, names, short phrases, and slogans; familiar symbols or designs; mere variations of typographic ornamentation, lettering, or coloring; mere listing of ingredients or contents.

- ideas, plans, methods, systems, or devices, as distinguished from a description or illustration.

- works that are designed for recording information such as blank forms, account books, diaries, address books, and the like.

- works consisting entirely of information that is common property containing no original authorship, such as standard calendars, height and weight charts, and lists or tables taken from public documents.

Can an Unpublished Book be Copyrighted?

Books, including short stories, poems, leaflets, narrative outlines, and periodicals, *cannot* be registered for statutory copyright protection in unpublished form. They secure statutory copyright by the act of publication with proper notice of copyright.

What Protection
Does My Unpublished Manuscript Have?

Prior to publication, your rights in your manuscript are protected under common law. This law arises automatically when the work is created. It requires no action in the Copyright Office, and lasts as long as the work is unpublished. In most cases common law gives you as much protection as a copyright. Once, however, the work is published, common law no longer protects it. If your work is published *without* the notice of copyright, it becomes public property.

Must I Apply for the Copyright Myself?

Either you or a duly authorized agent can apply for the copyright. The steps are relatively simple if you are familiar with the procedure.

Years ago, not being familiar with the steps involved in obtaining a copyright, I asked an attorney how much he would charge me to obtain a copyright for a book I was publishing. His answer was $50. I did not have an extra $50. Consequently the first edition of the book was not properly protected. Later, when the book was reprinted, still not knowing the law, I tried to copyright the second printing. The application was turned down. The book was in the public domain. I learned a valuable lesson.

Even though obtaining a copyright is relatively simple, you may not want to bother with the details. After all, you are a writer. Ask your printer for help. Most progressive book printers will perform this service for you as a part of their service. Because they do it so often, it becomes a simple task for them. Remember, however, that your printer is not a lawyer.

If you wish to file your own Application for Copyright, the information which follows will give you valuable advice. You will also find the Copyright Office is very helpful if you have specific questions. They may answer you with a form letter. I presume the same questions are asked over and over; but they *will* answer.

How Do I Go About Obtaining a Copyright?

Three steps should be taken to comply with the law concerning copyright in books.

1. *Produce the copies with the copyright notice in the proper form and position.* As a general rule, the copyright notice consists of three elements:

    (a) the word "Copyright," or the symbol "©." (Use of the symbol © may have advantages in securing copyright in countries that are members of the Universal Copyright Convention);

(b) the year of publication. This is the year in which copies were first placed on sale, sold or distributed by the copyright owner or under his authority;

(c) the name of the copyright owner or owners.

The three elements should appear together as follows on all copies: © 1975 by John Doe.

For a book, the copyright notice should appear on the title page or the page immediately following, which is normally the back of the title page.

2. *Publish the work.*

3. *Register your claim in the Copyright Office.* As soon as possible after publication, you should send:

(a) two copies of the book;

(b) a properly filled out, notarized, Application for Registration (For books, Form A, Class A, is the proper form for a book manufactured in the United states);

(c) a $6 check, money order or bank draft made payable to the Register of Copyrights. Don't send cash!

Mail the three items in a single package to the Register of Copyrights, Library of Congress, Washington, D.C. 20559.

You can also obtain the proper forms and request additional information from the same office.

How Should I Copyright
My Book if I Use a Pen Name?

You may copyright your work under a pseudonym, but it is also wise to include your full, legal name on the application.

How Long Does Copyright Protection Last?

The initial copyright in the United States runs for 28 years. The time begins on the date the work is published with the notice of copyright. A copyright may be renewed for a second period of 28 years if an acceptable renewal application and fee are received in the Copyright Office during the last year of the original term of copyright. For further information about copyright renewal write to the Copyright Office.

Any work published more than 56 years ago is in the public domain, which means it is no longer under copyright protection. If you do not renew your original copyright within the specified time, the copyright lapses and the works becomes public property.

Can a Copyright be Transferred?

A copyright may be transferred or assigned by an instrument in writing, signed by the owner of the Copyright. For information about assignments and related documents, request Circular 10 from the Copyright Office.

Do I Have Recourse if Some of My Material Was Originally Published without Notice of Copyright?

If a book has been published, printed or otherwise reproduced without notice of copyright, it is in the public domain. It is public property. The same holds true if you had a story or poem printed in a publication or anthology which was not properly copyrighted. If, however, your story was published in a newspaper, periodical, or book, bearing a *separate* copyright notice *in the author's name,* you already have the copyright and you should register it. If the publication itself was copyrighted, you may, by contractual agreement with the publisher, have the copyright to your story assigned to you after publication.

What Protection Does My Copyright Give Me in Foreign Countries?

The existing international copyright conventions give a U.S. citizen copyright protection in most important countries of the free world.

There are no special formalities required to obtain this protection, other than to use the symbol ©, which gives you protection in all countries which are members of the Universal Copyright Convention, followed by the year and name of copyright owner: © 1975 by John Doe.

To gain further protection, although it does not affect your U.S. copyright, the statement, "All Rights Reserved," placed directly below the copyright notice, will also comply with the requirements of all countries which belong to the Buenos Aires Convention—which includes the U.S. and most Latin American Countries.

If you have a specific question, address your inquiries to the Register of Copyrights, Library of Congress. For general information on this subject, request Circular 38.

Are Photographs and Artwork in My Book Protected?

The copyright covers all of the component parts of a book. Drawings, maps, photographs and the like, may *also* be *individually* copyrighted, whether published or not. Write to the Copyright Office requesting the proper forms.

Do I Need a New Copyright if My Book Is Revised or Reprinted?

A mere reprint of a book is not subject to a new copyright. The reprint should, however, bear the same notice of copyright that the first printing did. If the book is extensively revised, the revision may be copyrighted. In this case the book should bear the original copyright notice together with the new notice of copyright: "© 1972 by John Doe; revised edition © 1975 by John Doe," or "© 1972, 1975 by John Doe." The first copyright protects the original material; the second copyright protects only the portion which was revised.

Does the Copyright Office Act As a Law Enforcing Agency?

Although the copyright office will supply, free of charge, general information regarding copyright, and in certain cases make searches of claims after payment of a statutory fee, it does not give advice about the ownership of a copyright, getting a work published, obtaining royalty payments, or prosecuting possible infringers. The Copyright Office, in other words, does not practice law. If you have questions, it may be necessary to consult an attorney who deals with this phase of law.

How Long Does it Take for My Copyright to be Returned After the Application Has Been Sent?

From my experience, providing the Copyright Office does not question certain elements, it normally takes two to four weeks for you or your agent to receive your copy of the copyright registration form, bearing the registration number and the Copyright Office impression seal.

One advantage of having your printer or someone else familiar with copyright forms act as your agent, is that, because of their experience, it is easier for them to answer the questions which are often asked. Most often these relate to whether part of a book has been previously published elsewhere.

What Do I Do if I Have Further Questions?

Copies of the items listed below may be secured free of charge from the Copyright Office, Register of Copyrights, Washington, D.C. 20559.

> Form A, Class A (This is the proper form to be used for a published book manufactured in the U.S.)
> *General Information on Copyright*
> *Copyright Time Limits*
> *How to Investigate the Copyright Status of a Work*
> *International Copyright Relations, Including a Discussion of the Universal Copyright Convention*
> *Regulations of the Copyright Office*
> *Renewal of Copyright*

Other circulars on special subjects are also available on request. You will find the Copyright Office very helpful.

You may also consult the Bibliography in this book for books which will give you additional information.

16 HOW TO OBTAIN A LIBRARY OF CONGRESS CATALOG CARD NUMBER

Since 1901 the Library of Congress has, through its Card Division, made its printed catalog cards available to libraries throughout the world.

Since 1951 the Library has preassigned card numbers to forthcoming books. These numbers appear on the back of the title page of each book and are also included in the lists and reviews appearing in the leading journals of the book trade.

Use of the number enables subscribers to the Library's catalog card service to order cards by number and thus eliminate the searching fee.

Procedure for Securing Preassigned
Library of Congress Catalog Card Numbers

The Library of Congress card number must be requested *prior* to the publication of the book. Numbers are not preassigned to books that are already in print.

The publisher sends a request to the CIP Office, Library of Congress, Washington, D.C. 20540. The following information is needed:

1. Full name of author or editor
2. Title of the book
3. Edition statement
4. Date of publication
5. Name and address of publisher and/or printer
6. Series title and number
7. If a continuing serial (periodical, annual, conference proceedings, etc.)
8. If it is to be copyrighted
9. Approximate number of pages
10. Type of binding (hard, soft, etc.).

Are All Books Preassigned Numbers?

Catalog card numbers are preassigned only to books which the Library of Congress assumes it will add to its collections or for which it anticipates substantial demand for LC printed cards.

The types of material which the Library collects only in a very limited way and for which catalog card numbers are generally not available include: calendars, laboratory manuals, booklets of less than 50 pages, brochures, advertisements, bank publications designed for customers, blueprints, certain kinds of light fiction, privately printed books of poems, religious materials for students in Bible schools, catechisms, instructions in devotions, individual sermons and prayers, question and answer books, most elementary and secondary school textbooks, tests except for standard examinations, teachers' manuals, correspondence school lessons, translations from English into foreign languages, picture books, comic strip and coloring books, diaries, log and appointment books, prospectuses and preliminary editions, workbooks, and vanity press publications.

Upon examination, materials in the excepted categories may still be selected for the collections of the Library of Congress and cataloged. Accordingly, rejection of a work for preassignment of a number does not necessarily imply rejection from the collections.

The Library usually prepares only one card for serials, which in library parlance is called an open-entry card. The card number which is assigned to this card may be used for future issues of the serial. In general, because of internal problems in cataloging, the Library prefers not to preassign card numbers to periodicals.

Cataloging the Book

If the book is to be cataloged, a catalog card number is preassigned and sent to the publisher on a typed, three-by-five-inch temporary slip giving the author, title, imprint

---

Library of Congress Catalog Card Number: 75-12222

Mueller, L.W.
     How to Publish Your Own Book

Michigan   Harlo Press

1975   6'1'75

Temporary form issued by Library of Congress

and publication date. The catalog card number appears in the upper right hand corner of the slip.

The publisher prints this number on the back of the title page using the following wording: Library of Congress Catalog Card Number: 75-12222 (which is the number for this book). The first two digits do not indicate the year of publication, but the year in which the card number is preassigned.

The CIP office should be advised of all changes in titles, authors, etc., and cancellations. This notification is important as it prevents duplication of numbers. A new number is not necessary when changes are made. Confirmations of changes will not be acknowledged unless requested by the publisher.

Is There a Charge?

There is no charge for the preassignment of a card number. An *advance* complimentary copy of each publication should be sent to the CIP Office, Library of Congress, Washington, D.C. 20540. This copy is used for cataloging purposes so that cards may be printed before the book is released. The CIP Office provides postage-free mailing labels for use in sending these advance publications.

The Copyright Office is operationally separate from the CIP Office. A book may be copyrighted but not necessarily cataloged and added to the Library's collections.

Cataloging in Publication Program

Although this is not something you need concern yourself with if you are publishing only a single title, in 1971 the Library of Congress initiated an important new program called the "Cataloging in Publication (CIP) Program." Under this program publishers submit non-returnable galleys of their forthcoming books and a completed CIP data sheet.

Within ten working days after receipt, CIP data (including the Library of Congress catalog card number) is returned to the publishers for printing on the back of the title page. This service enables libraries to rapidly and economically process new titles for library users.

More information on this program is available from the CIP Office, Library of Congress, Washington, D.C. 20540.

Once a number has been assigned to a book, it will never be reassigned, even when the book is out of print.

17 HOW TO OBTAIN AN INTERNATIONAL STANDARD BOOK NUMBER (ISBN)

Since the middle 1960s, the book industry, like many other industries, has responded more and more to computerization.

In 1967, British publishers developed a Standard Book Number. This was adopted by American publishers in 1968. The following year the numbering system became an international standard, known as the International Standard Book Number (ISBN).

A "prefix number" is assigned to each publisher. This number is combined with a "suffix number," which identifies the title of the book. The ISBN for *this* book is 0-8187-0017-3. The 0-8187 is Harlo's prefix number; the balance of the number identifies the title.

Many U.S. publishers now participate in the program, placing the number on the back of the title page, at the foot of jackets, and on the spine of paperback books.

No doubt these numbers will be used more and more

in the future to streamline book ordering, but if you are only publishing one book, I'd say that the number is not mandatory.

If you wish more information, write to International Standard Book Numbering Agency, 1180 Avenue of the Americas, New York, N.Y. 10036. This organization will assign you a *Standard Book Number* and supply a Log Book that contains numbers for your specific use. Log Books vary in price, depending on the number of books you wish to list.

18 HOW LONG DOES IT TAKE TO PRINT AND BIND A BOOK?

If a printer or binder didn't have another job in his plant, the author lived near enough to the printer so he could read proofs immediately, and delivery time were eliminated, an average hardbound book could be produced in about three weeks. A more realistic time, however, is between sixteen and twenty weeks.

Many of the comments that follow are based on the average *hardbound* book. If your manuscript is to be produced as an unillustrated, thirty-two page, saddle stitched, or sixty-four page, perfect-bound book, the time would be less. If yours is a publication that repeats weekly, monthy or quarterly, and can thus be scheduled into the work flow, the time can be shortened even more.

Some of the comments which follow, however, apply to all books.

When you are aware of the number of details involved in producing a book, you will realize why it takes as long as it does. Let's take just one aspect of the overall production picture. By the time a printer marks up your manuscript, sets it into type, proofreads it, makes corrections, makes proofs, sends them to the author, makes corrections and changes as a result of the author's reading, makes the book into pages, makes proofs, sends them to the author for final reading and makes page proof corrections and changes, he has spent about an hour per page if the manuscript is simple.

If your book is 200 pages, that's 200 hours. At 40 hours per week, that's 5 weeks' work if only one person works on your book at a time. If the manuscript is complicated he could spend much more time.

Of course, more than one person is working on your book. Again, if the printer or binder didn't have any other work, one step would follow the other logically, without interruption.

Actually, because the printer is working on a number of books at one time, there is bound to be a time lag: The compositor is finishing typesetting another book, the proofreader is completing reading other proofs, the press—although it may take the pressman only a few hours to actually print your book—is tied up with other work.

Hardbinding is just as complex. Cloth has to be ordered, stamping dies made, folding completed, end sheets tipped on, books sewed, covers made and stamped. As with the actual printing, when various parts of the book finally reach the "line," the binding is completed in a short time.

It's very tempting for a printer and binder to promise what turns out to be an unrealistic delivery date. Perhaps when you first contacted him he was somewhat slack, so the date he promised was realistic. By the time he actually receives your manuscript, things may have changed. He has no way of knowing which of the many estimates he gives will result in actual orders. It's a very competitive field.

I've seen ads that guarantee a delivery date without even being able to examine a manuscript. I also know that these dates are not always met. Actually, the final determination of how long it takes to complete your book will be pretty much based on how busy the printer and binder are at the actual time they receive your work.

Following is a fairly realistic schedule for an average hardbound book of 192-320 pages:

Analysis, scheduling into work flow, styling	2 weeks
Composition (typesetting)	3 weeks
Reading galley proofs	1 week
Correcting galley proofs, reading corrections, making dummy, making into pages	2 weeks
Correcting page proofs, platemaking, and otherwise getting ready to print	2 weeks
Printing	2 weeks
Folding and binding	5 weeks
Total	17 weeks

To the foregoing must be added the days it takes for (1) the author to read galley proofs, plus the time spent in the mail going out and coming back; (2) the author to read page proofs, plus mailing time out and back; and (3) delivery of finished books to author.

Conservatively, these three factors will add another three or four weeks. To compound things even more, if proofs are not received by the time the printer thinks they will be back, he can't wait. He must keep his employees busy, even if it means that your job must be rescheduled. Believe me, it gets "hairy" at times.

There is another fact to bear in mind: When it comes to work days, a week is not seven days. It's five; forty hours, not counting overtime—which a lot of printers work but don't charge for.

There are also other incidentals that many people overlook. For instance, we often receive manuscripts that are not complete: The foreword is still being written, the author is checking facts on several pages, an illustration is coming. In some cases, even the manuscript or contract is not received when expected.

These things are normal in the printing industry and most printers accept the facts realistically.

On the other hand, authors and publishers should also take into consideration the unavoidable events that happen at the printer's end: The paper that was supposed to arrive Wednesday but didn't come until Friday; the plate that went bad and had to be remade; the stamping die that was promised in a week but took ten days; the book cloth that took four weeks to arrive instead of three; a machine that broke down and took three days to get repaired.

You must realize that there is much going on behind the scenes that you may not be aware of: frantic phone calls, overtime, the death of a key employee's father, the birth of a baby, a traffic accident, vacations.

I know it's frustrating if you don't know what's happening. You've spent God knows how many hours, even years, preparing your manuscript. You want your book by such and such a date.

By all means keep a thorough check on the progress of your work. But don't put all the blame on the printer and binder. After being in this business for over thirty years, I know many people in the industry. Most companies are honest and reliable and have the type of excellent, skilled workers that other industries would be proud to have. They are not necessarily giving you the run-around when they unavoidably miss a delivery date. More than likely they are working at their maximum capacity.

So don't schedule your delivery date too tightly. Give the printer and binder sufficient time to do a *good* job. Compare the total weeks, or years, you have spent completing your manuscript, checking to find the proper printer and getting estimates, with the *overall* time.

Be realistic. It may be more practical to set your publication date back and thoroughly exhaust the promotional possibilities that are discussed in Chapters 10 and 11.

And be happy your printer and binder are busy. It shows that other people *know* they are good. Just as important, maximum scheduling is the only way employees can be kept busy, and costs kept down.

19 THE PARTS OF YOUR BOOK

A book is normally divided into three parts: *preliminary pages, text,* and *end pages.*

Although your book may not contain all of the pages which are discussed, and some authorities disagree when it comes to placement of certain pages—and above all, tradition need not always be followed—I would suggest the following sequence of pages, particularly for a hardbound (case bound) book.

Remember, each sheet or leaf of paper contains two pages. The front of the sheet is a page; the back another. Left-handed (verso) pages are even numbered; right-handed (recto) pages are odd-numbered.

PRELIMINARY PAGES

End Papers

Although not a part of the written book, the end paper (which also appears at the back) is a four-page section of plain or printed paper which is a necessity in quality hard-bound books. It is, in effect, what holds the book together, as half is glued to the inside front or inside back cover, and the other half to the first and last page of your book. *Don't overlook it if you want an especially attractive book.* Normally white and unprinted, there is no reason why it need be white or cannot contain an attractive illustration.

Bastard Title or Half Title

The bastard title is usually the first printed page of a book. It normally consists only of the main title. Sometimes the main title also appears (particularly when preliminary material is extensive) just before the text. In this case it is referred to as the "half title."

Today, the term "half title," is often used interchangeably with bastard title. As one author says, "No doubt because of the delicacy of young women who work in the offices." (I must admit, however, that I nearly lost a customer one time when I referred to his "bastard title." He thought I was referring to the title of his book as being a bastard.) It is advisable to use a bastard title in a hardbound book because the end paper is glued to the first page, and thus it doesn't open completely flat. If your book is short, particularly if softbound, it can be eliminated.

Second Page (Back of the Bastard Title)

The second page is normally blank, but can contain a photograph, or the name of the editor if the book is one of a series. It is also proper to list other books published by the same author. In modern design, many books use the second page as an integral part of the title page, which follows.

Title Page

The title page lists the full title of the book, a subtitle if used, the name of the author or editor, a statement to the effect that this may be a revised edition or a second edition, and the name of the publisher. It is proper to insert a statement that your book has been privately printed, or you may use a name you have personally registered as the name for your publishing company.

Copyright Page

The copyright page is the page that gives your book protection. The copyright statement should contain the following: *Copyright* © *year, by,* and *the name of the copyright holder* (Copyright © 1975 by John Doe). If the symbol "©" is used, you may eliminate the word "copyright" (© 1975 by John Doe). Beneath this should appear the statement, "All rights reserved." You can also indicate the printing history (Fourth printing, 1975), if it is a reprint.

The copyright page is also the place to list the Library of Congress Catalog Card Number and International Standard Book Number (ISBN) if you have one. (Library of Congress Catalog Card Numbers, International Standard Book Numbers and how to obtain a copyright are discussed at length in other chapters.) If you are privately printing your book, you may also include the price of the book and your mailing address. At the bottom of the page you should state "Printed in the United States of America," or list the name and address of the printer.*

Dedication

Although called the "dedication page," you need not use the word. "To" is sufficient. The dedication, unless over a page in length, is normally followed by a blank page. Sometimes, in order to make the number of pages in a book come out even, or if the book is short, the dedication

---

*Most persons for whom Harlo produces books, allow us to insert a statement in small type at the bottom of the page to the effect that the book was "Printed by Harlo Press," and lists our address. Any correspondence or orders we receive are automatically forwarded to the author. We request that we be furnished with a number of stamped, self-addressed envelopes.

is placed on the back of the title page; otherwise it should be a right-hand page.

Epigraph

The epigraph consists of a pertinent quotation that sets the tone of your book. It need not be included, but if it is, it should be a right-hand page.

Contents

The contents page, which begins as a right-hand page, should include the title, chapter number and beginning page number of each section of the book. I would recommend the use of Arabic rather than Roman numerals for chapter headings. Roman numerals are somewhat of an anacronism. In poetry books, each poem is normally listed. Although your contents as typed will suit the *manuscript,* the *actual* page numbers will be inserted by the printer after he has made up the dummy for your book.

List of Illustrations

If your book is heavily illustrated, it may be wise to list the illustrations. Remember: *Illustrations sell books!* If your book has only a few illustrations—particularly if they are tied in directly with the text—this page (which should start as a right-hand page) need not be used.

List of Tables

If applicable, the list of tables should also be a right-hand page. It may also be appended to, or combined with, the page that lists illustrations. If the legend or caption which accompanies the text page is too long for proper listing in the preliminary pages, it may be shortened.

Foreword

A foreword is a statement made about the book by someone other than the author. It should start on a right-hand page and list the name of the writer at the end. The writer's title and/or affiliation may also be included.

Preface

The preface normally details the reasons why the author wrote his book, together with his methods of research. It should begin as a right-hand page and need not be signed. The preface should be relatively short.

Acknowledgments

If acknowledgments are few, they may be incorporated in the preface. If they are lengthy, they should start on a right-hand page. This page is commonly used to thank any individuals for help they have given you in the preparation of your manuscript, or permissions granted for the use of previously published work.

Introduction

In most cases I would recommend that the introduction, particularly when it actually sets the scene for the text, be a part of the text, rather than the preliminary pages. If, however, the introduction does not relate directly to the text, it should be included with the preliminary pages, starting on a right-hand page.

List of Abbreviations

Certainly not necessary in most books, the list of abbreviations should be included in books that contain many references to relatively few easily abbreviated sources. For easy reader reference, I would recommend that it be placed immediately preceding the text.

TEXT

Just as most paragraphs are made up of well developed sentences, and sentences of phrases, the text of your book should also follow a logical sequence. Only through planning can repetition be avoided.

Chapters

Works of prose are usually divided into chapters. The chapter title should give an honest clue to what the chapter contains. Many potential readers scan the table of contents to see whether the book might interest them.

Chapters should, if practical, be somewhat the same length.

The chapter number and title should appear at the beginning of each chapter. Generally, chapters begin as a new page. Most often they are brought down from the top somewhat. When books are short, it is common to start all chapters on right-hand pages, faced by a blank page if the previous chapter ended on a right-hand page.

Parts

If a book is extremely long or lends itself to *major* divisions, it can be divided into parts. The part number and part title normally begin on a new, right-hand page.

Subheads

Anything you can do to keep the reader's attention is important. Most people get weary when faced with extremely long chapters, as they do with extremely long paragraphs. I'd recommend keeping paragraphs short.

If chapters are long, particularly when material is complicated, it is wise to break the chapters with subheads. Subheads should be kept short and meaningful. In extreme cases you may need more than one level of subhead: a principal subhead (which, for instance, can be centered), and secondary subheads which can be set flush left.

Subheads, generally, are set as separate lines and need not be preceded by numerals or letters.

When your book is completed, a glance at the contents (with subheads included if you used them) will give you a word picture of your book, and point out inadequacies in logical progression.

Footnotes

Except where they actually clarify a portion of the text on a page, and even this type of clarification can often be written into the text, I would not recommend putting footnotes at the bottom of pages. It is considerably less expensive to arrange them numerically at the end of each chapter or at the end of the book by chapters.

Poetry

Most often, although not mandatory, each poem begins on a new page. If logical, a poetry book may be divided into parts. The part title (it need not be numbered) may be placed on a right-hand page preceding the group of poems, or it may be placed at the top of the first page of the group in a larger type face.

BACK MATTER

Appendix

Naturally not all books will have an appendix. If, however, the author wishes to elaborate on a portion of the text or substantiate facts, and the material is too long to put into footnote form, he may choose to place this material in the appendix. The appendix may also contain pertinent charts, tables and graphs. The first page of the appendix should start as a right-hand page. If more than one appendix appears, each should contain a number and title. Even though in some cases the appendix will appear in smaller type, it should be submitted to the printer double-spaced.

Notes

This page should start as a right-hand page and be arranged by chapter number and title. If extremely long, a smaller type size can be used, but you should submit your material double-spaced.

Glossary

When the reader is faced with foreign words or terms with which he is not readily familiar, a glossary can be especially helpful. The glossary should be arranged alphabetically and start on a right-hand page.

When assembling your glossary, I'd recommend going through the text page by page, listing any words or phrases you think may need clarification on a 3-by-5-inch card. After explaining the word, it is a simple matter to place the cards in alphabetical order. In all cases follow the same style throughout. Submit your glossary typed, double-spaced.

Bibliography

Although not all bibliographies follow the same style, be particularly careful to establish *one* style—and stick to it. The bibliography can be set in smaller type and should start as a right-hand page. You should submit it in double-spaced form.

Index

Nonfiction books, particularly if serious works, should have an index. It might be wise to refer to one or more of the books listed in the bibliography before attempting to prepare your index.

Although you can do preliminary work from your manuscript (place pertinent words on 3-by-5-inch cards in alphabetical order), the actual page numbers cannot be entered until the book is in page proof form. After you are sure everything is in order, it should be typed, double-spaced on an 8½-by-11-inch sheet. The index is normally set in smaller type, two columns per page, and begins as a right-hand page.

Colophon

Even though not used as commonly now as in previous years, I think a colophon adds a professional touch to a carefully designed and produced book. It details the production facts: book designer, type style, printer, paper, plate maker and binder.

20 WHAT TO DO WITH UNSOLD BOOKS

Like it or not, for one reason or another, some books don't sell—even when properly promoted.

It isn't anything to be ashamed of, since each year hundreds of books published by large companies have the same problem.

If you feel it's advantageous to unload your inventory, here are some suggestions:

You can prepare a mailer, offering your book at fifty percent off. As mentioned earlier, price is usually not the sole reason why people won't buy a book. So, before you go "whole hog," try a test to see whether it is worthwhile.

You can try selling your book in quantity to an organization, at an especially attractive price. Your library should have a copy of Gale's *Encyclopedia of Associations,* or a similar book which lists names and addresses of organizations.

You can be timid about admitting your failure and junk the books.

You can "remainder" the books.

Because of warehousing and bookkeeping costs, publishers often sell their slow moving books at a "close out" price to remainder dealers or book wholesalers. These companies, in turn, pass on this discount through their distribution system to the purchaser. It's a multi-million dollar business and can account for as much as one-third of a bookstore's gross.

As a sideline, there are a number of books that when once remaindered, have continued to be printed. I'm reminded of the case I read about, where a remainder dealer included a title on his list that sold so well, that he bought hardcover reprint rights from the publisher, and over a period of years sold over 250,000 copies of the book.

HOW TO REMAINDER YOUR BOOK

If you decide to remainder your book, write a letter to any of the listed companies which seem practical to you, stating what you have to sell. Include a copy of the book, or state that examination copies are available.

Indicate the quantity, the list price, whether the books are hardcover or paperback, their condition (perfect, slightly damaged), where the books are stored, and how they are packaged.

I suggest that you stipulate a closing date—say sixty days from the date of your letter.

At the end of this time, contact the highest bidder to be sure his offer still stands, and ask for shipping instructions. The bidder normally pays the shipping cost, but be sure to check this.

A & A Distributors, Inc.
Mear Road
Holbrook, Mass. 02343
Hardcovers and paperbacks

A & W Promotional Book Corp.
Attn: Lawrence D. Alexander
95 Madison Avenue
New York, N.Y. 10016
Large format pictorials

American Publishers Co.
1024 West Washington Boulevard
Chicago, Ill. 60607
All types of books in sheet or bound form

Book House
208 West Chicago Street
Jonesville, Mich. 49250
Hardcovers only

Book Sales, Inc.
110 Enterprise Avenue
Secaucus, N.J. 07094
Hardcovers only

Booksmith Distributing Co.
Attn: Barry Hockborl
1075 Commonwealth Avenue
Boston, Mass. 02117
Art, fiction, nonfiction, technical, crafts, childrens

Book Trading, Ltd.
102 Madison Avenue
New York, N.Y. 10016
*Juveniles, cook books, "How to," art and
photography*

Clearwater Books, Inc.
Attn: Mrs. S. Gooden
7 Island Street
Chippewa Falls, Wis. 54729

Gambler's Book Club
Attn: John Luckman
Box 4115
Las Vegas, Nev. 89106
*Books on gambling, casino games, horse racing,
poker*

Midwest Library Service
11400 Dorsett Road
Maryland Heights, Mo. 63043
Hardcovers only

Outlet Book Company
Attn: Joseph H. Reiner
419 Park Avenue, South
New York, N.Y. 10016
All types of books

Overstock Book Co., Inc.
Attn: Elliot Simmons
120 Secatogue Avenue
Farmingdale, N.Y. 11735
Will consider any type of books

Publishers Paperback Center, Inc.
3430 Croton Avenue
Cleveland, Ohio 44115
Paperbacks only

Quality Books, Inc.
Attn: Tom C. Drewes
400 Anthony Trail
Northbrook, Ill. 60062
Adult nonfiction, mysteries, westerns, art

S & L Sales Company
Post Office Box 579
Waycross, Ga. 31501
Hardcovers and paperbacks

Select A Book Corp.
163 Pennsylvania Avenue
Paterson, N.J. 07503
Paperbacks only

World Wide Book Service
251 Third Avenue
New York, N.Y. 10010
Paperbacks only

X-S Books, Inc.
675 Dell Road
Carlstadt, N.J.

21 A DISCUSSION OF "VANITY" PUBLISHING

We have a number of letters in our files from people who have had books "published" by "vanity" publishers. Here are extracts from two: ". . . I was 'victimized' for $4,000 by _____, who hasn't even tried to sell my books since . . ."; "I have written several manuscripts covering the supernatural . . . and anti-Semitism. I've been written up in *Who's Who*. . . . I got badly taken by subsidy publishers recently when I lost over $5,000, leaving me flat broke. . . ."

The methods for producing, promoting and marketing that I have discussed, assume that what you are actually doing is *publishing your own book*.

Great! You will realize after reading the news release issued by the Federal Trade Commission that they concur.

Their definition of a vanity publisher, coupled with their examples and recommendations, present an excellent summary of this method of "publishing."

NEWS RELEASE

FEDERAL   TRADE   COMMISSION

Washington, D.C. 20580

OFFICE OF INFORMATION   393-6800 Ext. 197

CONSUMER ALERT—THE VANITY PRESS

"The Federal Trade Commission today advised authors to proceed with caution and get the answers to some searching questions before contracting to pay 'vanity' publishers to have their books published.

"A vanity publisher is one who claims to furnish—for a fee paid by the author—all of the services involved in publishing a book including promotion and distribution. The cost to the author may range from $1,500 to $5,000 or more.

"An author who has met with no success in attempting to interest conventional publishers in accepting his book for publication is generally left with two alternatives. He can abandon his publication efforts and consign his manuscript to the closet shelf, or he can publish his own book at his own expense. There are two ways to do the latter. First, the author can personally arrange for the necessary editing, printing, binding and other steps and can publicize and distribute his own book. Second, he can contract for the services of a member of the vanity press.

"The Commission has no desire to interfere with the right of authors to publish their own books but it recommends that they be cautious when dealing with members of the vanity press. (Editor's Italics)

"In past years, the Commission has ordered a number of companies in this business to stop misrepresenting their services in many ways. Although these orders have effectively halted numerous misrepresentations, the Commission continues to receive complaints from frustrated and embittered authors who have undergone the frequently traumatic experience of having their books published by a member of the vanity press. These complaints do not suggest that there have been specific misrepresentations of the type prohibited by Cease and Desist Orders previously issued by the Commission. They do suggest, however, that before signing, authors should carefully consider the express provisions of the publishing contract and place less reliance on the publisher's promotional materials and representations.

"A typical complaint was from a disgruntled author who had paid $1,500 in advance for what he assumed was 3,000 bound copies and learned the hard way that the publisher was under no contractual obligation to print and *bind* that number. Upon the termination of his two year contract, few sales had been made and he asked the vanity publisher for the already paid-for unsold copies in stock. The publisher agreed to ship 290 bound copies and the remainder in flat sheets, and made this concession only after the author had threatened legal action.

" 'I did not pay $1,500 for thousands of sheets of paper,' the author lamented. 'Flat sheets would have to be bound. They are no good to me.'

"A literary agent made this statement to a poet who had had unfortunate dealings with a vanity publisher: 'I could have told you in advance that if any copies of the book were sold you would sell them yourself; these firms are not known for going out of their way to make sales.'

"This same poor but wiser author was also informed belatedly by a college journalism professor that 'you would have a better chance with reviewers and book stores if you published the book yourself and peddled it out of the back of your car.'

"The Commission recommends that an author seek and find answers to the following questions in order to be better prepared to consider whether he wants to sign a contract to pay for the publication of his book:

"(1) Am I counting on recovering all or a substantial part of my investment through the sale of my books?

"(2) If the book sells only a few copies, can I afford the loss of my investment?

"(3) If I contract for a specified number of copies of my book, will that number be printed and bound or is the publisher obligated to bind only those books for which a bona fide order is received?

"(4) Will the publisher deliver to me at no extra cost, all unsold copies of the book at the termination of the contract?

"(5) What do bookstores, book reviewers and librarians in my community think about books published by the vanity press?

"(6) Will I have to do most of the promotion of my own book?

"(7) Could I have my book edited, printed and bound locally for the same or lower charges than those quoted by the publisher?"

(Released January 14, 1970)

When a poet for whom we were producing a book discovered that I was compiling my thoughts, he sent the following:

NO SUBSIDIES—PLEASE!

"It was the fall of '73, I didn't go back to college— just couldn't hack it, and I wasn't sure what I wanted. So, as I was a bit lonely, I started to express my thoughts, my feelings, my emotions, in verse. And I very much enjoyed it.

"In about June of '74, I had enough poems to form a very tight, uniformed book, with a realistic theme— sure to sell, very appropriate photographs, threw in a pen-name to add a little mystery, and finally mailed a copy to myself for copyright protection.

"I sure felt cool! The only poetry writer in the area! Me, a poet! After my warm welcome from a subsidy press, I was just waiting to ride the train to glory, my ship to come in, etc., etc.

"I knew nothing about publishing, especially subsidy publishing. As far as I knew, making an 'investment' with a vanity press was how most people started—and it probably is, except they most likely do their first and last book with these 'outfits.'

"Like I said before, I knew nothing of the writing field. I figured it was an easy way to reach my 'claim to fame.' I found out the hard way, it was not.

"To make a long story short, the sad thing that I learned is that once a subsidy press gets your 'investment,' they don't care about your book—and why should they, they've got their money. You'll kill yourself trying to make your book 'catch on,' and they'll be making money, their primary concern, on the work that you do.

"After finding this information out—first hand, I simply wanted to quit. But I really couldn't. I realized that what local recognition I did get from my book was worth it, and quite simply, I enjoy expressing myself in verse.

"As a result, my second endeavor will be out soon with a private press, in which the books will be shipped to my house. I intend to move on, and hopefully pick up what I lost with my vanity press.

"The moral of this story is: Write because you enjoy it; there is no easy way to fame; and no subsidies—please!"

Of course, what could be called vanity publishing by a different name, occurs to a certain degree in large publishing houses. It would be economically unfeasible for even a legitimate publisher to reject a manuscript that can be turned into a saleable product, if someone wrote a history of a large corporation and promised to purchase 10,000 copies for his own use.

This is not necessarily bad, because most of the large publishers have standards. True, they might not have accepted the manuscript without the added incentive, but once accepted they will still apply their editorial and marketing expertise. More important, the author knows what it is going to cost him.

There are, however, some quite well known publishers who act in what could be referred to as a "grey zone."

Following is part of a letter from an author forwarded to us:

"Dear ——————,

"Your poetry manuscript ——————————— has been reviewed with a great amount of interest and we appreciate your sending it to us for consideration.

"COMMENT: 'Extremely well written poetry. The author writes in a free-flowing style that is most enjoyable. Many of these poems have previously been published and several have won prizes.'

"While our poetry reader has reported favorably on your manuscript, we must explain that most works of poetry need individual financing, either by the author or a sponsor. With the exception of poets like Sandburg, Nash, Armour, and a few others, there is, unfortunately, a relatively small demand for poetic works. In most cases the initial sales come from friends and relatives of the author. You will, therefore, secure the major portion of the sales. Since public demand is so negligible, book dealers generally show reluctance to carry the efforts of most poets, regardless of how good they may be. Therefore, it will be necessary that you underwrite publication of '—————————.' "

The author never did say what the charge would have been. At least the letter is honest. But why deal *through* someone else, when you can *publish your book yourself?*

To be fair, some of the vanity publishers have done a good deal of housecleaning lately. Their contracts are more specific; they answer questions more readily; they operate within their written agreements.

And, I'm not saying that books *can't* be successful if "published" by a vanity press. Some no doubt are, because they get repeat customers.

But we, as no doubt do other printers, produce books

for many authors who have gone the vanity press route previously.

Their chief complaint is that most of the sales were generated by them, not the vanity publisher. Their second complaint is high cost.

Their general feeling can be summed up as follows: If I'm going to do practically all of the work, why spend so much money, and why not receive the full amount from sales, rather than the "forty percent royalty" vanity publishers refer to.

So be careful. Read the fine print; know in advance what you can expect for your money.

If you don't believe me when I say to proceed with caution when dealing with vanity publishers, take the advice of the Federal Trade Commission.

22 OFTEN ASKED QUESTIONS

Can I write off the cost of self-publishing my book?

The best persons to consult for answering this question are your accountant or tax attorney. As I interpret it, publishing your book is a capital expenditure and any loss that may occur is a capital loss according to your tax bracket.

If you are ever audited by the IRS, however, be prepared to prove that you published your book with a profit motive in mind. Be sure to keep all correspondence and records of all income and expenses. Merely referring to your activities as a "business" is not enough.

Must I pay State Sales Tax on books I sell?

State sales tax regulations vary. Generally, books sold to individuals who live in your state will be taxable; if sold out of the state to individuals they will not be taxable. Sales to wholesalers and bookstores are normally not taxable because the tax is applied to the retail sale. Sales to registered non-profit organizations (schools, public libraries, etc.) are generally not taxable.

Your State Sales Tax Division will supply necessary information, and in order to avoid possible complications you should become thoroughly familiar with your responsibilities.

What constitutes copyright infringement?

This statute is rather vague and courts have been reluctant to define infringement. Generally, each case is dealt with individually. One test often used is to determine if the demand for the original work was lessened because of competition from the alleged infringement.

What constitutes libel?

American Heritage Dictionary defines libel as "any written or pictorial statement that damages a person by defaming his character or exposing him to ridicule." Legally, it's hard to define. Roberts Phelps and Douglass Hamilton wrote an excellent book called *Libel* (published by Macmillan), but if you have any questions you should consult an attorney.

How much can I quote without violation?

There appears to be no hard and fast rule. Under the doctrine of "fair use," you can quote from a copyrighted work to a limited extent, particularly for purposes of criticism or review. If you are in doubt, get permission from the copyright owner. If you cannot obtain it, avoid using it. Merely acknowledging that you are quoting from a copyrighted work, and naming it, does not constitute permission.

Do I have to get permission from authors if I am compiling an anthology or abridging work?

Compilations, such as anthologies, are regarded as new works and are subject to copyright law. An abridgment, if it results in a rewriting, is a new work of authorship and is also subject to copyright law. You must have written permission from the copyright owner in all cases.

How do I ask for permission to reprint or quote from a work that is copyrighted?

Make your request in writing. I'd suggest that the request be made in duplicate to the copyright holder. If you do not have his address, send it to him in care of his publisher. If you are granted permission the copyright holder can OK one copy and retain the other for his files. Make your request specific: List the exact title, exact page and then supply information about how you intend to use the information—in a book, periodical. Some publishers have their own forms which they will ask you to fill in and return.

What if I am asked for permission to reprint all or part of my work?

If you place your address on the back of the title page, requests may come directly to you. I've found, however, that many requests will come to the printer. We forward them automatically to the author, as will any legitimate printer. What you decide to charge, if anything, is up to you.

Can I copy, quote or extract material that appears in U.S. Government publication without fear of plagiarism?

Any material issued by the U.S. Government Printing Office that does not bear a copyright notice is in the public domain. You can use it without obtaining written permission.

Can I send my manuscript through the mails at a special rate or must I send it First Class?

Although I would recommend sending manuscripts by First Class Mail, registered if possible, there is a special fourth-class manuscript rate. This rate is discussed in Section 135.214F of the Postal Manual, should your Postmaster dispute it.

Must I pay postage when I send books to the Copyright Office along with the Copyright Application and fee?

No. Books may be sent free. If your local postmaster happens to be unfamiliar with the law, refer him to Section 137.22e of the Postal Service Manual.

Where can I find someone to type or retype my manuscript before submitting it for printing?

Both *Writer's Digest* and *The Writer* regularly list the names of individuals who perform this service.

23 GLOSSARY

Adhesive Binding. See *Binding.*

Alteration. See *Customer Changes.*

Antique. Paper with a surface that is neither polished nor coated.

Appendix. Material which follows the text of a book.

Backbone. See *Spine.*

Bastard Title. See *Half Title.*

Benday. A tone (10%, 30%, etc., of solid) applied to a solid. The process allows the printer to reproduce what looks like an additional color with a single pass through the press.

Binding. The various types of covering for the pages of a book, and the process involved in attaching the covers. Case (hard) binding, perfect binding, and saddle stitched binding are the most common. In *hard binding,* each signature is sewn through the middle fold with a thread which locks it at the back of the signature. It is then glued into position into the pre-prepared rigid cover, consisting of cloth-covered bindery board. *Perfect binding* enables the binder to hold books together without the necessity of sewing or stitching. Folded and collated, the backs of the signatures are cut off, leaving a roughened fiber surface to which the glue can adhere and to which the wrap-around paper covers are attached. *Saddle stitching* is a method whereby wire staples are pressured by force through the back fold of a booklet, stitched in the middle, enabling it to open flat.

Bleed. Extending the printed image to the very edge of the paper, eliminating all unprinted margins. An illustration can bleed top, bottom, left, right, or all four sides.

Blow Up. To enlarge photographically.

Body Paper. See *Book Paper.*

Body Type. Type used for the text of a book.

Book Cloth. Cotton cloth which has been sized or impregnated with pyroxlyn or other synthetic resins. It is available in white and many colors, finishes and weights.

Book Paper or *Body Paper.* A class of paper used for the main part of books, catalogs, etc. It comes in various weights, finishes and colors.

Bulk. Commonly used to indicate the thickness of a book, excluding the cover.

Camera-Ready Copy. Type, artwork, typewritten material, or the like, which is ready to be photographed for production without further work on the part of the platemaker.

Caption. Technically, the title appearing *above* a map, table, chart or illustration, as contrasted with a *legend,* which normally appears below. The term is *commonly* used for descriptive matter which appears in either location.

Case Binding. See *Binding.*

Clothbound. See *Binding.*

Coated Paper. Paper with an extremely smooth finish. It can have a glossy, *enamel,* finish or a *dull-coated* finish.

Cold Type. Generally, any process for setting type other than by the use of metal type. This can involve simple strike-on composition (typewriter), or complex, computer-driven photocomposition machines.

Collate. The assembly of single sheets or leaves into complete sets prior to binding. See *Gather.*

Compositor. A print shop worker who sets type.

Cover Paper. A paper made specifically for use as a cover of a book. It is available in various weights, finishes and colors.

Crop Marks. Marks that are placed on the edge or margins of drawings or photographs, indicating which areas are to be removed, and which serve as a guide to the cameraman.

Customer Changes. Any alteration of material after it has been typeset, not attributable to the printer's error and distinguished from a correction, is considered as a change and is normally billed separately, in addition to the charge for the original composition. See *Typographical Error.*

Cut. A plate used in letterpress printing.

Deckle Edge. Natural, rough edge of untrimmed paper as it comes from the machine.

Delete. Strike out, remove, or order to be removed.

Drop Folio. Page number at the bottom of a page.

Dummy. A "preview" of a book, normally made from the galley proofs which gives an indication as to the final appearance of a projected book.

Duotone. Halftone reproduction in two colors, made from original black and white copy.

Dust Jacket. See *Jacket.*

Ellipsis. Equally spaced periods indicating the ommission of a word, line, phrase or paragraph in quoted matter.

Enamel. A glossy, coated paper.

End Paper. The folded sheet of paper, attached to the first and last signature of a book, which, in turn, is glued to the inside front and back cover of a case bound book.

Engraving. A general term applied to any printing plate made by an etching process used for letterpress printing.

Face. A style of type.

Flat. Positives or negatives stripped into position on a masking sheet the size of the printing plate, prior to making plates for offset printing. Also used to indicate a paste-up of a number of pages prior to making a negative.

Flush. Term used to indicate the absence of indentation. *Flush left* means that the lines are to begin at the left margin; *flush right* lines align at the right margin.

F.O.B. Literally "free on board." In actual practice it means that the customer pays for all shipping.

Folio. Page number.

Format. Appearance of the book, as determined by size, shape, margins, printing requirements, etc.

Four-Color Process. Sometimes called "four-color printing," this technique enables a printer to reproduce an infinite range of colors through the use of black and variations of the primary colors: red, blue and yellow.

Galley. See *Proof*.

Gather. Placing folded signatures in their proper sequence, prior to being bound.

Grain. The direction in which the fibers run in a sheet of paper.

Gutter. The inner margins of facing pages in a book.

Half Title. A brief title, usually the only thing printed, on the first page of a book and sometimes on the page immediately preceding the text.

Halftone. A printing plate made by a photographic and chemical process, in which the photograph, printing or other continuous-tone copy, is broken down into a series of very small dots.

Hanging Indention. Type set with the first line flush left and the rest of the lines indented. The type in this *glossary* is set in this manner.

Hard Binding. See *Binding*.

Head. A word or phrase used to divide books into chapters or sections. Also the top of a page.

Headband. A decorative band used at the top and bottom of the spine of a quality hardbound book.

Inferior Number or *Letter*. A small number or letter used in formulas (11_3), etc., that prints below the alignment of normal letters. See *Superior Number*.

Initial Letter. A large, decorative letter used to begin a chapter or section of a book.

Intertype. A line casting machine similar to the Linotype.

Italic. A sloping version of a type: *Italic* type.

Jacket. Sometimes called a "dust jacket." The paper cover folded over a bound book, which is used for protection and advertising a book.

Justify. To equally space out words in a line of type, so that lines come out even at both ends.

Layout. The working diagram of a page or book. It shows spatial area, and spacing of text, illustrations, etc.

Leader. An evenly spaced row of dots or dashes which guide the reader's eye across the page.

Leading. Spacing added between lines of type.

Letterpress Printing. Printing from a raised surface, such as type, border material or photo-engravings.

Ligature. Two or more letters combined to make a single piece, such as fi, ff, fl, ffi, ffl, etc.

Line Drawing. A drawing which contains no grays or middle tones. The type of drawing that can be done with pen and ink.

Linotype Machine. A typesetting machine developed in the late 1800's. By touching individual keys on a keyboard, matrices combine to form words. These matrices are then justified, come in contact with molten lead, and form an entire line called a *slug.*

Lithography. See *Offset Printing.*

Lowercase. Small letters, as distinguished from capital letters.

Measure. The length of a line.

Numerals. Arabic numerals: 1, 2, 3, 4, 5, etc.; Roman numerals: I, II, III, IV, V; i, ii, iii, iv, v, etc.

Offset Printing. A printing method whereby an image, design or page is reproduced photographically onto a metal plate. The plate is then attached to a revolving cylinder of a printing press. The reproduced material from the metal plate is transferred to a rubber blanket which, in turn, transfers, or offsets it onto the paper.

Opacity. In printing paper, the desirable quality which prevents the showing through of printed pages.

Outline Halftone. A halftone from which most of the background has been eliminated.

Overrun. Copies printed in addition to those actually ordered. As it is virtually impossible for a printer to print and bind the exact number of copies ordered, most contracts allow for a five or ten percent over- or under-run.

Page. One side of a leaf or sheet. Each leaf or sheet contains two pages. The pieces of paper which go into the making up of a book.

Page Proof. See *Proof.*

Paper Weight. The weight of 500 sheets of a certain basic size of paper. This book is printed on 60 pound book paper.

Pasteup. Assembling copy for photographing by placing all type, illustrations, etc., into their proper place.

Perfect Binding. See *Binding.*

Photocomposition. See *Cold Type.*

Photo Offset. See *Offset Printing.*

Pica. Twelve points. Approximately 1/6 of an inch.

Plate. A thin, flexible, metallic plate from which the image is transferred from plate to blanket to paper in offset printing. See *Engraving.*

Point. .01384 inch. A type measurement. Approximately 1/72 of an inch.

P.P.I. The number of pages that it will take any given paper to bulk up to one inch in thickness.

Proof. A reproduction of the type after it has been set, which has been proofread and checked for errors. *Galley Proof:* The first proof taken of copy after it has been set, a copy of which is sent to the author who, along with the printer, can check for machine errors, which are corrected and inserted while the type is still in galley form. *Page Proof:* A reproduction of the type, made up into page form, which is also sent to the author for a second checking for errors. *Revised Proof:* A new impression of galley and/or page proofs after corrections have been made and inserted.

Public Domain. Not protected by copyright.

Pyroxlyn. Cellulose nitrate material (plastic) used for impregnating or coating book cloth.

Recto. A right-hand page.

Reproduction Proof. See *Proof.*

Retouching. Improving original artwork by hand prior to making plate.

Reverse. A printing process whereby what would ordinarily print as color, prints out as white, and what would ordinarily print as white, prints in color. In this way, the white or color of the paper can be utilized as a "color."

Revised Proof. See *Proof.*

Reverse Plate. A plate in which the parts that are usually black or shaded are the opposite, or reversed, so as to appear white.

Running Head. Title repeated on consecutive pages of a book. Usually, if used, the title of the book appears on even numbered (left-hand) pages, the chapter title on odd-numbered (right-hand) pages.

Saddle Stitching. See *Binding.*

Scaling. The process of calculating how large an illustration will be after cropping and reducing or enlarging. Also an accurate estimate of how many pages a manuscript will print out as.

Scoring. Putting a crease in paper, so it will bend more readily.

Sheet. Two printed pages—one on *each* side of a leaf of paper, is called a sheet.

Signature. A section of the book normally obtained by folding a single sheet of paper into 16 or 32 page sections.

Silverprint. A photographic print on paper which has been sensitized. The printer uses silverprints to give his customer a general idea of how the finished job will look.

Skid. The quantity of paper or finished books that can be packed conveniently on a moveable platform. Usually no more than 2500 pounds.

Slug. A line of type or spacing material cast from a Linotype or similar machine.

Solid. Type matter with no leading added between lines.

Spine. That part of the book which is visible to the eye when stored on a shelf and upon which the title, name of author, and publisher usually appears.

Stamping. Reproducing a design or title on a book cover, using metal foil, colored foil, or ink.

Stock. See *Paper.*

Strip. To combine one photographic negative with others, preparatory to making a plate.

Superior Number or *Letter.* A small number or letter that prints above the alignment of normal letters, often used to indicate footnotes.[3]

Tint. A light color or the light color obtained by breaking the solid color into a series of dots, thus enabling the printer to produce what looks like more than one color in a single pass through the press.

Tip-in. An individual leaf, printed separately, which is pasted, or tipped, into the book.

Trim Size. The size of the finished item after it has been trimmed. The normal trim is ⅛ inch.

Typewriter Composition. Material typed upon a typewriter, usually with "book" typefaces, on a variable spacing typewriter, for reproduction.

Typographical Error. An error made by a typesetter. Not the customer's fault.

Verso. A left-hand page.

Wash Drawing. A brushwork drawing that contains grays. See *Line Drawing.*

Widow. A short line ending a paragraph and appearing at the top of a page. Widows are unsightly and the careful printer avoids them by adding or deleting space.

24 IMPORTANT ADDRESSES

This is not a complete list, but every person who is seriously interested in writing should subscribe to one or both of the following magazines:

Writer's Digest, 9933 Alliance Road, Cincinnati, Ohio 45242. Published monthly; $7.95 per year.

The Writer, 8 Arlington Street, Boston, Mass. 02116. Published monthly; $9.00 per year.

If you want to get a general feeling of the publishing industry, subscribe to or thoroughly examine issues of all or part of the following magazines:

Publishers Weekly, 117 Church Street, Whitinsville, Mass. 01588. Published weekly; $25.00 per year. *This is the publication that most booksellers subscribe to. Along with advertisements of forthcoming books, it forecasts what the editors feel will be good sellers, lists best-sellers, and tells the story of publishing on a week-to-week basis.*

Book Production Industry, 21 Charles Street, P.O. Box 429, Saugatuck Station, Westport, Conn. 06880. Published bimonthly; $10.00 per year. *This magazine is distributed to personnel actually engaged in book publishing, design and manufacturing. It contains a lot of information of general interest.*

There are also a number of publications which should be available for reference purposes in your local library or which you may wish to purchase.

AB Bookman's Yearbook. Antiquarian Bookman, Box 1100, Newark, N.J. 07101. *This is issued annually.*

AD Guide—An Advertiser's Guide to Scholarly Publications. American University Press Services, Inc., One Park Avenue, New York, N.Y. 10016. *A marketing reference and guide to editors of specialized journals.*

All-in-One-Directory, R. R. Bowker Co., 1180 Avenue of the Americas, New York, N.Y. 10016. *Listing of thousands of public relations outlets in all media.*

American Book Trade Directory, R. R. Bowker, P.O. Box 1807, Ann Arbor, Mich. 48106. *A comprehensive directory which lists names and addresses of booksellers in the U.S. and Canada, private book clubs and dealers in foreign language books.*

American Library Association Membership Directory, American Library Association, 50 East Huron Street, Chicago, Ill. 60611. *Lists names and addresses of over 31,000 members.*

American Library Directory, R. R. Bowker Co., 1180 Avenue of the Americas, New York, N.Y. 11036. *Detailed listing of American and overseas libraries.*

Associated Church Press Directory, Associated Church Press, 326 West State Street, Media, Pa. 19063. *Lists complete Protestant magazines and newspapers in U.S. and Canada plus some Catholic and Orthodox publications.*

Ayer Directory of Publications, Ayer Press, West Washington Square, Philadelphia, Pa. 19106. *Complete listing of address, editor, publisher, circulation, advertising rates, size, etc., for most publications in the U.S., Canada, and surrounding territory.*

Books in Print, R. R. Bowker Co., 1180 Avenue of the Americas, New York, N.Y. 10016. *Expensive. Lists by author and title thousands of books currently in print.*

Broadcasting Yearbook, Broadcasting Publications, Inc., 1735 DeSales St. N.W., Washington, D.C. 20036.

Contemporary Authors, Gale Research Co., Book Tower, Detroit, Mich. 48226. *Has listed and is continuing to list, thousands of authors together with biographical information. After you have published your book, by all means let them know about it.*

Directory of College Bookstores, B. Klein Publications, Box 8503, Coral Springs, Fla. 33065. *Pretty good if this is your field. Lists several thousand college bookstores and tells whether they are college or privately owned.*

Directory of Mailing List Houses, B. Klein Publications, Box 8503, Coral Springs, Fla. 33065. *Names over 2,000 list houses, specialists and brokers.*

Directory of Syndicated Features, Editor and Publisher, 850 Third Avenue, New York, N.Y. 10022. *An alphabetical listing, by title, of features, authors, classifications, etc.*

The Editor & Publisher International Yearbook, Editor and Publisher, 850 Third Avenue, New York, N.Y. 10022. *Lists daily and weekly newspaper data and addresses.*

Educational Directory, One Park Avenue, New York, N.Y.
    10016.

Encyclopedia of Associations, Gale Research Co., Book
    Tower, Detroit, Mich. 48226. *An invaluable guide to
    over 14,000 national organizations in the U.S. Most
    categories are covered.*

Forthcoming Books, R. R. Bowker Co., 1180 Avenue of
    the Americas, New York, N.Y. 10036. *Issued bi-
    monthly, this publication lists by author and title, all
    books scheduled for publication in the coming five
    months.*

International Yearbook, Editor and Publisher Co., 850
    Third Avenue, New York, N.Y. 10022. *Complete list-
    ing of newspaper personnel, advertising agencies, and
    other worthwhile information.*

Kirkus Reviews, 60 W. 13th Street, New York, N.Y. 10011.

Library Journal, R. R. Bowker Co., 1180 Avenue of the
    Americas, New York, N.Y. 10036. *Contains reviews
    of current books recommended by the editors.*

Literary Market Place, R. R. Bowker Co., 1180 Avenue of
    the Americas, New York, N.Y. 10016. *Issued annually,
    this is probably the most important single source of
    reference for any person who publishes a book. It lists
    agents, artists, associations, book clubs, book reveiwers,
    exporters and importers, magazines, newspapers, news
    services, radio and television, services such as typing,
    shipping and translators . . . and much more.*

Ulrich's International Periodicals Directory, R. R. Bowker
    Co., Box 1807, Ann Arbor, Mich. 48106. *Lists by title,
    publisher, subscription rate, and frequency of publica-
    tion, more than 61,000 periodicals.*

Writer's Handbook, The Writer, Inc., 8 Arlington Street,
    Boston, Mass. 02116. *Issued annually, this excellent
    reference book lists over 2,000 sources for manuscript
    sales plus other valuable information.*

Writer's Market, Writer's Digest, 9933 Alliance Road, Cincinnati, Ohio 45242. *Good. Contains much excellent information.*

Writer's Yearbook, Writer's Digest, 9933 Alliance Road, Cincinnati, Ohio 45242. *Includes general and specific information on writing, markets, etc.*

25 BIBLIOGRAPHY

Ashley, Paul P. *Say It Safely: Legal Limits in Publishing, Radio, and Television.* 3d ed. Seattle and London: University of Washington Press, 1966.

Bartlett, John. *Familiar Quotations: A Collection of Passages, Phrases, and Proverbs Traced to Their Sources in Ancient and Modern Literature.* Edited by Emily Morison Beck. Boston: Little, Brown & Co., 1968. *This book, which incidentally was originally self-published, is the source to consult when checking familiar quotations.*

Bingley, Clive. *The Business of Book Publishing.* Pergamon Press: New York, 1972. *This book has excellent background material but much of the information is slanted toward the British rather than the American publisher.*

Bogsch, Arpad. *The Law of Copyright Under the Universal Convention.* 3d ed. New York: R. R. Bowker Co., 1969.

Carey, Gordon V. *Making an Index.* Cambridge Authors' and Printers' Guides, no. 3. 3d ed. Cambridge: At the University Press, 1963.

Collison, Robert L. *Indexing Books,* Rev. ed. Tuckahoe, N.Y.: John de Graff, 1967.

Curl, Peter. *Designing a Book Jacket.* New York: The Studio Publications, 1956.

Dessauer, John P. *Book Publishing: What It Is, What It Does.* New York: R. R. Bowker Co., 1974.

Fowler, H. W. *A Dictionary of Modern English Usage.* 2d ed. revised by Sir Ernest Gowers, Oxford: Clarendon Press, 1965.

Gaskell, Philip. *A New Introduction to Bibliography.* New York: Oxford University Press, 1972.

Henderson, Bill. *The Publish-It-Yourself Handbook.* Yonkers, N.Y.: The Pushcart Book Press, 1973. *A collection of experiences by a number of people who have published their own books.*

Huenefeld, John. *How to Make Money Publishing Books.* Bedford, Mass.: Vinebrook Publications, Inc., 1974. *A comprehensive guide and reference for managers of small book publishing houses.*

The Huenefeld Report. Bedford, Mass.: Perspective Press, Inc. *A worthwhile fortnightly four-page newsletter dealing with various facets of publishing. Back issues are available.*

Jennett, Sean. *The Making of Books.* New York: Frederick A. Praeger, 1967. *Good, illustrated, overall view of publishing and book manufacturing.*

Kent, Allen, ed. *Copyright: Current Viewpoints on History, Laws, Legislation.* New York: R. R. Bowker Co., 1972.

Lee, Marshall. *Bookmaking, The Illustrated Guide to Design and Production.* Ann Arbor, Mich.: R. R. Bowker Co., 1965.

Nicholson, Margaret. *A Manual of Copyright Practice: for Writers, Publishers, and Agents.* 2d ed. New York: Oxford University Press, 1956.

Olsen, Udia G. *Preparing the Manuscript.* New York: The Writer, Inc., 1972.

Schwartz, Robert J. *The Complete Dictionary of Abbreviations.* New York: Thomas Y. Crowell Co., 1955.

Skillin, Marjorie E. and Gay, Robert M. *Words into Type.* Englewood Cliffs, N.J.: Prentice-Hall, Inc., 1974. *Very good.*

Spiker, Sina. *Indexing Your Book: A Practical Guide for Authors.* Madison: University of Wisconsin Press, 1953.

Strauss, Victor. *The Printing Industry, An Introduction to Its Many Branches, Processes and Products,* Ann Arbor, Mich.: R. R. Bowker Co., 1967.

Turner, Mary C. *The Bookman's Glossary,* 5th ed. New York: R. R. Bowker Co., 1975. *Good description of terms used by printers and publishers.*

United States Government Printing Office. *Style Manual.* Washington, D.C.: Government Printing Office. *This covers style as practiced by the Government Printing Office. Excellent treatment, but I would recommend* A Manual of Style, *published by the University of Chicago Press.*

University of Chicago Press. *A Manual of Style.* Chicago: The University of Chicago Press, 1969. *Highly recommended.*

Updike, Daniel Berkeley, *Printing Types: Their History, Forms, and Use.* Cambridge, Mass.: The Bellknap Press of Harvard University, 1962.

Webster's Biographical Dictionary: A Dictionary of Names of Noteworthy Persons with Pronunciations and Concise Biographies. Springfield, Mass.: G. & C. Merriam Co., 1956.

Webster's Geographical Dictionary: A Dictionary of Names and Places with Geographical and Historical Information and Pronunciations. Springfield, Mass.: G. & C. Merriam Co., 1966.

Webster's New Collegiate Dictionary. Springfield, Mass.: G. & C. Merriam Co., 1975.

Webster's New International Dictionary of the English Language, Unabridged. Springfield, Mass.: G. &. C. Merriam Co. *This is the* big *book. If it is out of your price range, I'd recommend* Webster's Collegiate Dictionary.

Williamson, Hugh. *Methods of Book Design.* 2d ed. New York: Oxford University Press, 1966.

Wittenberg, Philip. *The Law of Literary Property.* New York and Cleveland: World Publishing Co., 1957.

*This book and jacket were designed
by Marion Mueller
and printed by Harlo Printing Company.*

*The text type—11 point on 12 Times Roman—
was set by Linotype.*

*The headline type, jacket copy and captions
were composed on a
Compugraphic Unified Composer
and set photographically on an ACM 9000
in various sizes of Univers type.*

*The text paper is an off white, sixty pound,
offset paper, supplied to Harlo's specifications.*

The printing was done by offset lithography.